Essays in Memory of Christine Burleson

Essays in Memory of

Christine Burleson

in language and literature by former colleagues and students

Edited by Thomas G. Burton

RESEARCH ADVISORY COUNCIL
East Tennessee State University
Johnson City, Tennessee

TYPOGRAPHY, PRINTING, AND BINDING IN THE U. S. A. BY
KINGSPORT PRESS, INC., KINGSPORT, TENNESSEE

❋ *❋* *❋* *❋* *❋* *❋*

A pristine blossom engendred by learning,
No fragile flower sterile in art,
But bountiful as the Lady-Slipper,
In eternal summer blooms.

—T. G. B.

Contents

Miss Christine Burleson's eminence is perhaps no more clearly revealed than in the following statement she wrote near the end of her life upon receiving the East Tennessee State University Distinguished Faculty Member Award:

President Dossett and Colleagues:

Long years ago (in 1917 to be exact) the faculty of East Tennessee State Normal School honored me by selection as one of four students appearing on our Commencement Program. Now, just fifty years later, I proudly acknowledge what is the highest honor of my entire lifetime. It comes when destiny has ended my career of teaching, at least for awhile.

As you know, our profession is one of maximum challenge and opportunity. No other could provide anyone with more opportunities for personal growth and enrichment. Every period spent in a classroom has given me a sense of exhilaration, of enjoying human fellowship, and of getting inspiration from the finest possible sources. Furthermore, nowhere in this world could one enjoy better associations than with a group of teachers. My father taught me a prayer by Socrates which ended:

Fifty years ago, "May I consider the wise to be the wealthy, and may I have such a quantity of gold as only the temperate can bear."

Tonight you have bestowed upon me such a quantity of gold that I shall be counting it over to the very end, bewildered, dazed, but utterly happy because the best of all rewards has come to me. I thank you all!

Christine Burleson

Chronology

1899   —Born January 5 in Florence, Alabama, the younger daughter of David Sinclair and Mary Henley Dew Burleson.

1905   —Entered Training School of State Normal School (Florence, Alabama), beginning in the second grade.

1911–1917—Attended East Tennessee State Normal School, passing over the eighth grade to begin with high school pupils; received diploma in 1917. Activities included participation in basketball, school orchestra, and student publications.

1914   —Baptized May 6, First Christian Church, Johnson City, Tennessee.

1917–1919—Attended the University of Tennessee. Activities included being a sponsor of the band (1918); a staff member of the school newspaper, the *Orange and White* (1918–1919); Associate Editor of the yearbook, the *Volunteer* (1919); a member of *Le Cercle Français*, the Women's Student Literary Club, and Chi Omega (chosen as one of Chi Omega's twenty-five nationally outstanding women). Elected to Phi Kappa Phi Honor Society in 1918 and received A.B. degree, *magna cum laude*, in 1919.

1919–1920—Attended Vassar College as a senior; received B.A. degree in 1920.

1920–1921—Studied as a graduate student in philosophy and English at Columbia University.

1921–1925—Taught English and science at Kemper Hall, Kenosha, Wisconsin.

1923   —Spent summer in Italy.

1925   —Completed thesis and other requirements for M.A. degree during the summer term at Columbia University.

1925–1927—Taught at East Tennessee State College.

1927–1928—Did educational research for Westchester County Children's Association, New York.

1928   —Entered Lady Margaret Hall, Oxford University; continued studies there and took Honors B.A. in English Language and Literature in 1931.

1931–1932—Studied during the winter at Siena, Italy; received certificate in Italian from the University of Siena in 1932.

1932–1936—Served as Dean of Women and Professor of English at Bethany College, West Virginia.

1936–1946—Taught for father, "approximately a year's substituting," and assisted him in two series of widely adopted texts, grades 3–8, published by Allyn and Bacon, *Adventures in Language* (1934–1938) and *Adventures in English* (1939–1944, rev. 1947 and 1952)—of the latter series, joint author of Grade 3 (1952 ed.), Grade 6 (1952 ed.), Grade 7 (1947 and 1952 eds.), Grade 8 (1944 and 1952 eds.). Other activities included numerous speaking engagements.

1937   —Taught spring term at the University of Tennessee.

1939   —Received *in absentia* M.A. degree from Oxford.

1946–1967—Taught English language and literature at East Tennessee State University, including a wide scope of both undergraduate and graduate courses, but with special concentration in Shakespeare; activities included re-peated attendance at Shakespeare festivals (Antioch, Ohio, and Stratford, Ontario) and membership in the Monday Club Auxiliary, Monday Club, and Fortnightly Club.

1967 —Received on September 15 the first annual Distin-guished Faculty Member Award.

—Died November 2 in Johnson City, Tennessee, after teaching—in positions from student-teacher to professor —during every decade of the University's existence.

Behind "The Minister's Black Veil"

John D. Allen

EAST TENNESSEE STATE UNIVERSITY

That the heritage of Puritanism shaped importantly the artist in Nathaniel Hawthorne, no informed person would question; and for a good many seasons in the classroom I had suggested not only that in his story "The Minister's Black Veil" the reflection of that influence is evident but also that the symbolism of the veil is clear. I had supposed, and said, that it represents the dogmas so powerfully and rigorously expounded by John Calvin: predestination, original sin, total depravity, eternal punishment for all but a handful of human souls elected for glory by an angry Jehovah. I had assumed that episodes in the brilliantly dramatic tale dramatize the implications of those dogmas for the human condition, for human relationships. And I had inferred that the tale expresses Hawthorne's rejection of Calvinistic theology, fascinating though its consequences were to him as materials for literary art.

For support of this interpretation of the veil, it had not occurred to me that perusal of scholarly reflections might be desirable. Granted that Hawthorne is sometimes equivocal, even obscure, it had nevertheless seemed that moderate acquaintance with the history of New England, reasonably firm grasp of the tenets of Calvinism, fair knowledge of the temperament and the predilections of the author as man, and some capacity for appreciating the subtleties of a very fine but not very mystifying artist —it had seemed to me that this modest equipment ought to be and had been adequate to remove the crepe from the countenance of the minister without assistance from scholar or critic, who, I assumed, had no doubt already done or concurred in the deed.

In this confident faith I was disturbed some years ago by an experience connected with a master's thesis which I had been asked to read. The thesis included interpretations of the symbolism in six of Hawthorne's tales, among them "The Minister's Black Veil." For it the author presented an exposition that violated my sense of the credible; and a suggestion that the story be re-examined elicited only a parroting of the text. With no intention to apply an academic cudgel, I decided, however, to search out the source from which the cherished jewel had been filched, with results that momentarily shook faith in my ability to tell symbols from handsaws. My travels in Hawthorne territory did not, of course, exhaust the sights. But the thirty or more books and articles which appeared to view probably constituted a fair cross-section of the titles that might be expected to touch on the particular tale; and the twelve which mention it probably exhibited the range of published commentary bearing on the narrative. When I had turned the last page, I was reduced to the disconcerting knowledge that not one of the twelve advanced the interpretation which to sophomores I had long been casually uttering.

Troubled by the loneliness, I decided to re-examine the story in the hope that I might discover an overlooked piece of evidence to support my view. I found it, and to me it seemed and still seems conclusive. What this evidence is, will be set forth later in this paper. In the meantime, the reader may find useful a summary of the fiction, which will be followed by a resumé of the interpretations encountered during my course of reading.

One Sabbath morning the Rev. Mr. Hooper appeared in the pulpit of colonial Milford's meeting-house with his face shrouded in black crepe. The phenomenon startled the congregation, evoked a variety of speculations, lent force and terror to a sermon on secret sin. Later in the day, Hawthorne tells us, the veil seemed "an appropriate emblem" at the funeral of a maiden, between whom and her pastor some relationship is ambiguously suggested; and still later it cast a pall of horror over a wedding ceremony. Subsequently it alienated the minister's fiancée; and, unable to wean Mr. Hooper from what the author calls "so dark a fantasy, which if it had no other meaning, was perhaps a symptom of mental disease," she renounced marriage and re-signed him to the veil.

And behind the veil Mr. Hooper steadfastly journeyed through a long and useful life, to rationalists a harmless eccen-tric, to the multitude a bugbear—"irreproachable," Hawthorne comments, "in outward act, yet shrouded in dismal suspicions; kind and loving, though unloved, and dimly feared; a man apart from men, shunned in their health and joy, but summoned to their aid in mortal anguish"—in process of time a famous preacher, "a man of awful power over souls that were in agony for sin." And, the veil still unlifted, in time he came to die. "Why do you tremble for me alone?" he cried with his last breath to those gathered about the couch. "I look around me, and, lo! on every visage a Black Veil!"

So runs the narrative, one of the most finished and least equiv-ocal productions, it seems to me, of a fine craftsman and very fine artist.

Probably the first published comment on the story was the brief mention by Edgar A. Poe, to whom it also seemed excellent in quality, but not at all ambiguous. The minister and the dead maiden had been partners in an act of genital commerce, a con-clusion not explicit in Poe's magisterial remarks but surely therein implied.[1] In view of his morbid interest in dead ladies, it is easy to imagine how he reached it. Three pieces of evidence might well have provided clues.

One piece, the subtitle "A Parable," assures reader and critic that the veil has symbolic meaning. The second, Hawthorne's

---

[1] Review of *Twice-Told Tales*, by Nathaniel Hawthorne, *Graham's Maga-zine*, May 1842.

footnote, tells him what not to infer. It mentions an historical clergyman who, having accidentally killed a friend, thereafter hid his face from mankind. It adds merely that in that case "the veil had a different import." The import of the fictional minister's veil, Poe must have inferred from the third piece of evidence, Hawthorne's account of the maiden's funeral, the only part of the narrative that conceivably might support Poe's thesis. I quote two crucial passages:

> As he stooped, the veil hung straight down from his forehead, so that, if her eyelids had not been closed forever, the dead maiden might have seen his face. Could Mr. Hooper be fearful of her glance, that he so hastily caught back the black veil? A person who watched the interview between the dead and the living, scrupled not to affirm, that, at the instant when the clergyman's features were disclosed, the corpse had slightly shuddered, rustling the shroud and muslin cap, though the countenance retained the composure of death. A superstitious old woman was the only witness of the prodigy . . . .
>
> "Why do you look back?" said one in the [funeral] procession to his partner.
>
> "I had a fancy," she replied, "that the minister and the maiden's spirit were walking hand in hand."
>
> "And so had I at the same moment," said the other.

These passages are obviously important, but do they compel the inference which Poe evidently drew from them? In my opinion, they do not. They might, in fact, be satisfactorily explained by reference to the predilection of Hawthorne for dabbling his toes in the murky waters of the supernatural. How strong this predilection was, one may learn from the essay on "Hawthorne's Supernaturalism" in Prosser Hall Frye's out-of-print volume *Literary Reviews and Criticisms*, published in 1908. Frye does not mention "The Minister's Black Veil," but observations such as the following might well breed skepticism regarding the soundness of Poe's judgment:

> In this general derangement of [the New Englander's] moral world former lines of demarcation became gradually blurred or

wholly obliterated, until its ill-defined boundaries ceased at last to oppose an obstacle to the intrusion of impertinent and superstitious fancies. And it is this crumbling—or rather this shrinking away—of the old faith from its original metes and bounds, together with the laying bare of that visionary borderland between wind and water, between reality and illusion, which is represented by Hawthorne's dusky chiaroscuro, streaked with the shadow of things imperceptible by direct vision and filled with the air of mysterious and invisible wings. (pp. 124–125)

In devising the funeral scene, however, Hawthorne perhaps was doing more than yielding to the mesmerism of the supernatural, or indulging a flair for employing it to create atmospheric effects. Perhaps he was hinting that from the unCalvinistic realm it now inhabited, the spirit of the maiden (like the spirit of the minister's betrothed) looked with horror on a face behind which lurked a monstrous obsession. Or perhaps he meant to suggest that the minister was himself appalled by the embodied death before him—by this visible evidence of the workings of Jehovah's will—and that, dismayed by the apparent cruelty of a Creator who, in punishment for Adam's sin, could consign to physical decay and eternal vengeance the maiden grace and loveliness before him, Mr. Hooper clutched the veil in superstitious terror before an eye that might open and, in opening, accuse and condemn. And if, to superstitious observers, there seemed to be a secret affinity between the spirit of the dead maiden and the living minister, perhaps Hawthorne meant to intimate that, for the superstitious, the affinity would be original sin, through whose operation spirit and spirit might well be fancied by a Calvinist as walking to the cemetery hand in hand. Certainly there is no need to assume that the minister is a prototype of Arthur Dimmesdale. Nor, it would appear, has any later critic or scholar accepted Poe's notion that the veil symbolizes deplorable carnal behavior.

Much more attractive has been the opinion expressed by George E. Woodberry in his biography of Hawthorne, published in 1902. Hawthorne, he asserts,

7

uses the veil to typify man's concealment of himself from others, even the nearest; and while it visibly isolated the minister among his fellow-men, it finally unites him with them in a single lot; for to the mind's eye . . . all men wear this veil; humanity is clothed with it in life, and moulders away beneath it in the grave, whither its secrets are carried.[2]

Of course the veil conceals, isolates, unites. But by failing to see it as the symbol of Calvinism, which he nowhere relates to the story, Woodberry is able to achieve no more than a timid and distorted glimpse of the truth.

This theme of isolation may be detected in Amy Louise Reed's article "Self-Portraiture in the Works of Nathaniel Hawthorne," published in 1926. There, however, as the title suggests, it is applied to Hawthorne himself. Miss Reed reaches what she admits to be "the somewhat fantastic conclusion that Hawthorne's young heroes and his mature villains are compounded of the same materials and that both are varieties of self-portraiture." She adds that Hawthorne himself had a sense of personal guilt, that in many of his stories characters are hiding "a painful secret," and that Mr. Hooper hides one (she does not choose to say what) behind the veil.[3]

Newton Arvin apparently agrees in the main with Woodberry and Miss Reed, though he does not appear to credit Hawthorne with cherishing some secret, some personal guilt. Discussing a group of tales of which "The Minister's Black Veil" is one, he says in his study of the author, published in 1929:

> The essential sin, [Hawthorne] would seem to say, lies in whatever shuts up the spirit in a dungeon where it is alone, beyond the reach of common sympathies and the general sunlight. All that isolates, damns; all that associates, saves.[4]

[2] *Nathaniel Hawthorne* (Boston and New York, 1902), pp. 145–146; see also p. 149.
[3] *Studies in Philology*, XXIII (January 1926), 51–52.
[4] *Hawthorne* (Boston, 1929), pp. 59–60.

Mr. Arvin, who offers more to the same effect, sounds like one of the earlier evangelists of the gospel of togetherness.

Despite his contributions to Hawthorne studies, the late Randall Stewart has hardly succeeded in removing Mr. Hooper's veil. In his valuable edition of Hawthorne's *American Notebooks*, published in 1932, he, too, follows Woodberry in saying that the minister "had committed no peculiar sin" and that "the black veil symbolizes a degree of concealment, or lack of complete openness of heart, common to all mankind." [5] This emphasis reappears in his study of Hawthorne, published in 1948.[6] In short, with reference to this story his view remained substantially that of Woodberry. Ten years later, however, although he does not mention "The Minister's Black Veil" in his volume *American Literature and Christian Doctrine* (Baton Rouge, 1958), he does unequivocally assert that "The concept of Original Sin runs through all of Hawthorne" (p. 79).

In the meantime Malcolm Cowley, using a shotgun loaded by Freud, had aimed to blast the veil from the minister's—and his creator's—face. Cowley's Introduction to *The Portable Hawthorne*, published in 1948, informs that after the author was "happily married," he was able to "look back almost tranquilly on his autoeroticism. . . . But some of the stories that Hawthorne wrote in the Salem days—I am thinking especially of 'Young Goodman Brown' and 'The Minister's Black Veil'—so testify to his sense of guilt that they might have been cries from a convocation of damned souls" (p. 10). Mr. Cowley would seem to possess an enviably delicate gift for extra-sensory perception of clandestine behavior-patterns cultivated by authors many years ago. After him, Mark Van Doren perhaps felt that the veil might better be left alone. Brief comment in his biography of Hawthorne, dated 1949, closes with this informative observation:

[5] "Introduction," *The American Notebooks by Nathaniel Hawthorne* (New Haven, 1932), p. xlvi *et seq.*
[6] *Nathaniel Hawthorne, A Biography* (New Haven, 1948), pp. 257–258.

The veil "obscurely typifies" some mystery [Hawthorne] lets Mr. Hooper say. Obscurely, yes. But even the mystery is obscure.[7]

Richard H. Fogle, in a study of Hawthorne's fiction published in 1952, devotes eight pages to painstaking analysis of the story but seems unable to achieve conviction as to its author's intention. He moves cautiously toward the correct interpretation of the veil as symbol when he says that Mr. Hooper "is Everyman, bearing his lonely fate in order to demonstrate a tragic truth."[8] He quickly skips away, however, to grasp the familiar theme of isolation, with its implication of some weakness or taint in Mr. Hooper's character.

Briefly in his volume *Hawthorne's Faust*,[9] published in 1953, and at length a year later in an article for *American Literature*,[10] William Bysshe Stein advances probably the most novel interpretation of the tale thus far proposed. The article is entitled "The Parable of the Antichrist in 'The Minister's Black Veil.' " Mr. Hooper is the Antichrist; and, according to Mr. Stein, every one of his actions is a satanic parody of one or another of the precepts for the good shepherd set forth or implied by the Apostle Paul in First and Second Corinthians. Though Mr. Stein does not employ the exact words, one is encouraged to think of the conduct of the benign Mr. Hooper as constituting an epical analogy, extended over a lifetime, to the ceremony of the Black Mass.

So much for the fruits of my reading in quest of authoritative support for an amateur's opinion. The effort had not been wasted; for I had incidentally learned much about Hawthorne from scholars and critics who ignore the story, and perhaps something from those whose explications I had examined, without being persuaded to accept them. As I have said, I returned to

[7] *Nathaniel Hawthorne* (New York, 1949), p. 87.
[8] *Hawthorne's Fiction: The Light and the Dark* (Norman, Okla., 1952), pp. 33–40.
[9] Gainesville, see pp. 3–4 and 80–81.
[10] XXVII (November 1955), 386–392.

the tale, where after close reading I found conclusive evidence, it seems to me, for my own interpretation. At the end of a long paragraph about the great power and wide fame of Father Hooper's preaching, Hawthorne remarks with characteristic casualness that, during the administration of Governor Belcher, the minister was appointed "to preach the election sermon" at an annual gathering of the colonial court.

Now, Belcher was governor of Massachusetts and New Hampshire between 1721 and 1742, dates which help to place in historical time Mr. Hooper's fictional career; and during that period much the most important movement in New England was what historians call the Great Awakening. Here then, it would seem, was the unobtrusive but plain and compelling clue to the symbolism of the veil. I had overlooked its significance before. So, apparently, had the Hawthorne critics and scholars.

Elaborate correlation of the clue with features of the story would require much space and would seem hardly desirable here. I must be content with restatement of my thesis, followed by brief comment on a few points that perhaps have given rise to muddy exegesis.

The black veil does, as I had supposed, symbolize Calvinism, the total depravity and alienation from Jehovah which Calvinism posits for all but a handful of Adam's children; but it symbolizes something more specific. Mr. Hooper's donning of the veil symbolizes the Great Awakening, that belated and shortlived but tumultuous revival in a decorous and decadent Calvinism for which the saintly Jonathan Edwards was the most famous, the most lovable, the most brilliantly and consistently logical exponent. The story reflects Hawthorne's clear-eyed analysis of the movement and, I believe, his rejection of the theology it expressed. Incidentally, though one need not insist that Edwards was the original of Father Hooper, obvious analogies between the two exist.

The character of Elizabeth, the minister's betrothed, may have puzzled some of the commentators. Doubtless she speaks to some extent for the author, as Mr. Fogle believes; but perhaps she is intended as a reflection of something more. Contemporary with Jonathan Edwards were minds with the temper of Benjamin Franklin's—minds practical, earth-centered, disposed to worship not Jehovah but a benevolent, if remote, deity who could be counted on to approve man's struggle to achieve goodness through his own effort and ingenuity. Perhaps Elizabeth (as do lesser characters in the story) speaks for them. Like them, a village Franklin in skirts could have loved the person and spirit of a Jonathan Edwards, of a Mr. Hooper, but would have been repelled to the point of renunciation by what, in the fictional character, his betrothed suspected to be the strange and gloomy obsession of an unbalanced mind.

Near the end of the story a young minister tries to induce his elder to permit removal of the veil and is shocked by the convulsive vigor with which the dying man resists the effort and clutches the veil to his countenance. The implications are obvious. Would a firm Calvinist deny with his last breath the faith by which he had rigidly lived, on which he had based his hope for eternal bliss? And would not a young pastor, less rigorously schooled in Calvin's gloomy doctrines, perhaps even dubious of their validity, be startled by the fierce tenacity of a soul about to face its Maker?

One other point: Hawthorne quickly moves on in the narrative from the funeral scene to the wedding. By thus linking those two profoundly important events—the one closing, the other leading to, life—does he not deftly imply that the black veil of Calvinism cast a pall of gloom over the whole creation? By such frugality of means is a great artist able to achieve subtlety and depth of expression.

If space permitted, other passages in the tale might be cited in support of the interpretation I have advanced. Nothing, I believe, opposes it. I must leave the story, however, to the reader's imagination and judgment, confident that he will see what I see behind the minister's black veil.

Tennyson's *Ulysses* and Translations of Dante's *Inferno:* Some Conjectures

Edgar Hill Duncan

VANDERBILT UNIVERSITY

It is generally recognized that Tennyson borrowed from Dante's *Inferno,* Canto XXVI, the setting and incident which provide the dramatic situation for his poem *Ulysses.* Paull F. Baum has demonstrated conclusively the dependence of one poem on the other by quoting passages from Dante alongside parallel passages from Tennyson.[1] Critics also agree that there is here no servile imitation of the earlier by the later poet—that Tennyson's *Ulysses* as poem and portrayal of the hero therein set forth are uniquely Tennyson's own creation. Not all recent critics have, however, been happy with the result. Friedrich Brie, in 1935, Douglas Bush, in 1937, W. H. Auden, in 1944, W. B. Stanford, in 1954, and Clyde Ryals in 1964 have all found faults more or less grave in the poem; and Professor Baum, in an appendix to his book on Tennyson, 1948, has delivered the most thorough and devastating attack on it.[2] I have attempted in a paper published ten years ago to answer Professor Baum's charges.[3] I mention this fact because what I shall conjecture in the present paper depends, in part, on the interpretation of the poem I have suggested in the former one.

Briefly stated, my contention is that Tennyson's portrayal of Ulysses is not an attempt at an objective delineation of the character of Ulysses, the epic hero, but rather an appropriation

[1] *Tennyson Sixty Years After* (Chapel Hill, 1948), pp. 92–95.
[2] Baum, pp. 299–303.
[3] "Tennyson: A Modern Appraisal," *Tennessee Studies in Literature,* IV (1959), 13–30.

on the young poet's part of that character as a symbol of a powerful drive in his own mind. The poem is an adumbration of an immediate and, as it proved, temporary resolution of a debate between two concepts of the poetic function which were striving for mastery in Tennyson's mind. The one, represented by Ulysses in the poem, conceives of the poet as *oracular*—as capable of discovering hitherto unapprehended truths by exploring the depths of his own psyche—and of the function of poetry as the pursuance of this aim.[4] The other, represented by Telemachus, conceives the poet's function as social, educative, normative, didactic. Such earlier-written poems as *The Mystic, The Poet, The Poet's Mind, The Hesperides,* and the sonnets entitled *Life* and *To Poesy* among others are evidence of Tennyson's preoccupation with oracular poetry. The critics of his first two volumes and a majority of his friends urged him to write the other kind. F. D. Maurice, J. S. Mill and, most importantly, Arthur Hallam believed in the oracular mode and strongly urged Tennyson to pursue that. The whole debate was intensified in Tennyson's mind as a phase of his reaction to Hallam's unexpected death; *Ulysses* was written within a month after that event.[5]

If the interpretation of the poem as a symbolic presentation of Tennyson's mental debate is correct, we should expect a use of the kind of imagery in portraying Ulysses, as opposed to Telemachus, which would be symbolically representative of the psychic activities of an oracular poet. And we are thus provided with a point of view from which to conjecture Tennyson's appropriation of the Ulysses passage in Dante's *Inferno.* Ob-

[4] For the term *oracular* and its application to poems of the early 1830's see Robert Preyer, "Tennyson as an Oracular Poet," *Modern Philology,* LV (1958), 239–251.

[5] Hallam died in Vienna, September 15, 1833; Tennyson learned of his death on October 1 (Charles Tennyson, *Alfred Tennyson* [New York, 1949], p. 144). The version of *Ulysses* in J. M. Heath's Commonplace Book is dated October 20 (Charles Tennyson, "Tennyson Papers," *Cornhill Magazine,* CLIII [1936], 438). An even earlier version is in Harvard Notebook 16 (George D. Marshall, *A Tennyson Handbook* [New York, 1963], p. 95).

viously inappropriate would be Dante's conception of the soul of Ulysses as suffering in hell for his wiliness and wrath which had caused the death of Achilles as well as the capture of the Palladium. Also inappropriate would be Dante's conception of Ulysses' final earthly sea-journey as "foolish" (*folle*) and of his physical death as resulting from a tempest rushing upon his boat from the mountain-island of Purgatory. All of this Tennyson silently omitted. On the other hand, Ulysses as continual seeker and as voyager in unknown seas would obviously be appropriate to such a conception; and these aspects form the staple of Tennyson's portrayal.

I want now to explore the possibility that in developing specific images from this basic figure of Ulysses as seeker and voyager Tennyson might have been influenced, whether consciously or unconsciously, by English translations of the Dante passage which were known to him. How well, in his twenty-fourth year, he could read Dante in the original I have been unable to discover. A program of private study which he drew up some months after Hallam's death included Italian, German, and Greek as subjects for the afternoons of successive weeks.[6] Hallam's intensive study of Italian literature, especially Dante, and his accomplishment in the language were no doubt partly responsible for Tennyson's interest.[7] But, as several of his adolescent poems seem to indicate, Tennyson knew Dante's poems before meeting Hallam.[8]

As to English versions of the *Inferno*, there were no fewer than six in existence at the time Tennyson composed his poem.[9] Henry Boyd's translation of the *Inferno*, published in 1785, was

[6] Hallam Tennyson, *Tennyson: A Memoir* (London, 1897), I, 124.
[7] Charles Tennyson, *Alfred Tennyson*, pp. 64–65.
[8] Charles Tennyson, p. 32.
[9] The earliest, 1782, is by Charles Rogers, *Inferno* only. This was followed by Henry Boyd, *Inferno*, 1785, *Comedy*, 1802; H. F. Cary, *Inferno*, 1805, *Comedy*, 1814; Nathaniel Howard, *Inferno*, 1807; Joseph Hume, *Inferno*, 1812; Ichabod C. Wright, *Inferno*, early 1833. Boyd's and Wright's are in 6-line stanzas, the others in blank verse (Gilbert F. Cunningham, *The Divine Comedy in English: A Critical Bibliography, 1782–1900* [New York, 1965], pp. 13–45).

in his father's library. Cary's translation of the *Inferno* was published in 1805 and his translation of the whole of the *Divine Comedy* in 1814 with new editions in 1819, 1822, and 1831. It is inconceivable that Tennyson did not know it. My evidence indicates that he may also have read the version of the *Inferno* by Nathaniel Howard which was published in 1807. The other three versions can be safely dismissed. But I suggest that the three named ones, especially Boyd's and Cary's, may be at least as important as the original in the background of the poem *Ulysses*. For I conjecture that one or another or all three of them provided suggestions toward the phrasing of several particular images in a more immediate way than the Italian original could possibly have done. Cary's and Howard's versions are in blank verse. They are considerably more faithful to the original, in the Ulysses passage and throughout, than Boyd's, which is in stanzas of iambic pentameters riming aabccb.

I should like to examine six items from the poem in this connection:

1. "I cannot rest from travel; I will drink Life to the lees" (lines 6–7.
2. The "arch" passage, lines 19–21.
3. Every hour as a "bringer of new things" (line 28), with which is associated the "newer world" of line 57.
4. "To follow knowledge like a sinking star" (line 31).
5. "To sail beyond the sunset, and the baths Of all the western stars" (lines 60–61).
6. ". . . the gulfs . . ." (line 62).

It will be best to begin with the "sinking star" of item 4, which shows the clearest dependence on Boyd. "What precisely is a *sinking* star?" Professor Baum asks, somewhat impatiently.[10] Whatever it is, the hint for it may possibly have come from two passages in Boyd's version:

> The broad Atlantic first my keel impress'd,
> I saw the sinking barriers of the west . . . . (XVIII, 1–2)

[10] Baum, p. 300.

> 'Till ev'ry well-known star beneath the deep
> Declin'd his radiant head . . . . (XX, 2–3) [11]

There is nothing in Dante which exactly corresponds to the second line of the first passage. In the relevant place (after the mention of Spain, Morocco, and the island of Sardinia), Dante has: "E l'altre che quel mare intorno bagna" (line 105),[12] which the Carlyle-Wicksteed translation renders: "and the other islands which that sea bathes round."[13] Cary translates: "and each isle beside / Which round that ocean bathes" (lines 103–104).[14] The important point is that Boyd has completely dissociated his line, both syntactically and by stanza division, from Sardinia, and has thus left "barriers" to be interpreted as a reader wishes. Tennyson, connecting with the later passage, seems to have associated the "barriers" with stars. The later passage, using the verb "declin'd," conveys the idea of *sinking* in a way not quite suggested by the original or by Cary:

> Dante: Tutte le stelle già dell' altro polo
> Vedea la notte, e il nostro tanto basso
> Che non surgeva furor del marin suolo. (lines 127–129)
> Cary: Each star of the' other pole night now beheld,
> And ours so low, that from the ocean-floor
> It rose not. (lines 123–125)

Boyd reverses the order, thus emphasizing the *sinking:*

> 'Till ev'ry well-known star beneath the deep
> Declin'd his radiant head; and o'er the sky
> A beamy squadron rose, of name unknown . . . .

If the process of association was initiated as the young Tennyson mused over Boyd's lines, the "sinking star" image could have

---

[11] *A Translation of the Inferno of Dante Alighieri in English Verse* (London: Printed by C. Dilly, 1785). The episode is in Vol. II, pp. 222–226. Boyd numbers the stanzas; I add line numbers within stanzas.

[12] *La Divina Commedia,* ed. C. H. Grandgent (New York, 1909). The episode is on pages 210–214.

[13] Modern Library Edition (New York, 1932). The episode is on pages 142–144.

[14] *The Vision . . . of Dante Alighieri* (London: Taylor and Hessey, 1819). The episode is on pages 228–231.

been further intensified by Nathaniel Howard's translation of Dante's "Tutte le stelle" tercet:

> . . . soon th' Antarctic pole
> Blaz'd with the fires of night, while lowly sank
> Our starry watch beneath the marble sea.[15]

It will be more convenient to look at other items before considering the "knowledge" which is associated in item 4 with "sinking star." That knowledge is, I think, a profound extension of the knowledge yearned for in Tennyson's earlier sonnet entitled *Life:*

> Would I could pile life on life, and dull
> The sharp desire of knowledge still with knowing! [16]

Yet the mood- and word-echoes of these lines in our item 1, "I cannot rest from travel; I will drink / Life to the lees" and in "Life piled on life / Were all too little" (lines 24–25) have prompted a recent critic to characterize this sonnet as having in it "the germ of *Ulysses*." [17] And they encourage a subjective interpretation of the later poem. Boyd's version is closest in mood to these lines:

> . . . nor aged sire
> Nor son, nor spouse, could check the wild desire
> Again to tempt the sea, with vent'rous oar (XVI, 4–6),

both in the vividness of "wild desire," for Dante's "l'ardore," Cary's "zeal," and Howard's "ardour," and in the decided reduction of the roles of father, wife, and son in purveying a contradictory mood. Cary and Howard, following Dante closely, give full force to the claims of these three. Cary translates:

---

[15] *The Inferno of Dante Alighieri Translated into English Blank Verse* (London: John Murray, 1807), p. 159.

[16] *Memoir*, I, 59.

[17] D. B. MacEachen, "Tennyson and the Sonnet," *The Victorian Newsletter*, No. 14 (Fall, 1958), p. 5.

Nor fondness for my son, nor reverence
Of my old father, nor return of love,
That should have crown'd Penelope with joy . . . . (lines 93–95)

And Howard:

Nor sweet affection for an infant son,
Nor reverence for an aged sire, nor love
That should have blest Penelope with joy . . . . (page 158)

Tennyson goes even farther than Boyd, dropping out the father altogether, bringing in the son later in his poem for another purpose,[18] and giving to Penelope, nameless as in Boyd, Boyd's and Howard's epithet for the father: "aged wife" (line 3).

I am not sure that the "arch" image of lines 19–21 owes any indebtedness to Dante. Professor Ryals has recently wondered whether there may be a connection between this "arch" and the "double arches" of a juvenile poem, which Tennyson never published, through which the narrator sees lying "Fair with green fields the realms of Love." "Are those double arches," Professor Ryals asks, "the same image as the metaphor of experience which the poet employs in *Ulysses?*" [19] He does not carry his speculation beyond asking the question, doubtless because of the vast difference in theme and situation, at the relevant point, between the two poems. In the earlier one, the youthful narrator wandering amid mountain scenery catches through double arches a glimpse of Ideal Love. In the latter, an aged sea-wanderer images his own limited, though enormously rich, experience as an arch which tantalizingly reveals the infinite nature of Experience itself. If the carry-over of the *arch* owes anything to Dante's lines, Boyd's translation would seem to be the effective vehicle, for his version comes closer to suggesting such an image than does the original. It is a matter of verbs. Dante's *terza* is built on the single verb *saw:*

[18] For a discussion of the function of Telemachus in the poem, see my paper cited earlier.
[19] Clyde de L. Ryals, *Theme and Symbol in Tennyson's Poems to 1850* (Philadelphia, 1964), pp. 110–111.

21

L' un lito e l'altro vidi infin la Spagna,
Fin nel Morrocco, e l'isola de' Sardi,
E l'altre che quel mare intorno bagna. (lines 103–105)

Boyd, varying the verbs, brings in both movement and curvature:

I circled round the Celtiberian strand,
I saw the Sardian cliffs, Morocco's land,
And pass'd Alcides' straits with steady gale. (XVII, 4–6)
The broad Atlantic first my keel impress'd,
I saw the sinking barriers of the west . . . . (XVIII, 1–2)

It is at least possible that "circled round" may have suggested the arch; if so, Cary's rendering of Dante's last clause, "Which round that ocean bathes" may have reinforced the image, as also Howard's "Bath'd by the circling ocean" (page 159). Again, Boyd's "sinking barriers of the west" may lie behind Tennyson's "untravell'd world whose margin fades . . ." (line 20). As a possible hint for the first two words, Boyd offered "new worlds unknown to mortal view" (XVIII, 6) and Cary: "the unpeopled world" (line 114), for Dante's "del mondo senza gente" (line 117).

Items 3 and 5 are so intimately bound up with the following of "knowledge" of item 4 in the contexture of Tennyson's poem that the three must necessarily be considered together. The "new things" of line 28 (item 3) is a looking ahead to the "new world" of line 57, which is to be sought "beyond the sunset, and the baths / Of all the western stars," lines 60–61 (item 5), a quest worthy to occupy the energies of the speaker "until I die." And these are in turn metaphors for the psychic travail of the oracular poet expressed in item 4:

To follow knowledge like a sinking star,
Beyond the utmost bound of human thought. (lines 31–32)

The particular cluster of images associating in this poem a "new" kind of knowledge, in the sense of something esoteric or beyond the commonly known, with the *west* is not a new thing for Tennyson. He had already developed the symbol, as J. Robert Stange has shown, in his poem *The Hesperides*, published in the 1832 volume.[20] *The Hesperides* is the most elaborate of Tennyson's poems written in the oracular mode. It is largely devoted to an incantatory development of the symbolism of the west as the home of "all good things" and contains the packed image: "the treasure / Of the wisdom of the West," as signifying both the cause and the subject of oracular poetry. I conjecture that this west symbolism has been carried over into *Ulysses*, that in fact it is precisely the voyaging in western seas which most powerfully attracted Tennyson to Dante's lines. If so, the three translations could have reinforced the appropriateness of the carry-over. In addition to the general geographical location, Dante employs three specific references to *west:* "all' occidente" (line 113) and "Diretro al sol" (line 117); he indicates the direction of Ulysses' sailing by "E volta nostra poppa nel mattino" (line 124). Cary renders the three respectively as "to the west" (line 110), "following the track / Of Phoebus" (lines 114–115), and "to the dawn / Our poop we turn'd" (lines 121–122). Howard translates them: "coasting now the west," "Follow the sun," and "Our stern . . . to the rising morn" (p. 159). Boyd does not translate any of these directly; but in his condensed adaptation of Dante's lines 124–135 the third becomes positively expressed: "Since first the western surge receiv'd our prow" (XXI, 3), and the approximate place of the first is filled by his most striking line: "I saw the sinking barriers of the west." There are thus eight distinctive western images in the three translations as compared to three of the original.

Dante's second *west* image, which is part of his reference to the "world without people behind the sun,"[21] Boyd renders: "And find new worlds unknown to mortal view" (XVIII, 6). It is this line which, as I conjecture, could have linked the image

---

[20] "Tennyson's Garden of Art: A Study of *The Hesperides*," *PMLA*, LXVII (1952), 732–743.
[21] Diretro al sol, del mondo senza gente. (line 117)

"new worlds" to "knowledge" for Tennyson; and the oracular quality of that knowledge is suggested in Cary's rendering. Cary has Ulysses address his companions:

> ". . . refuse not proof
> Of the unpeopled world, following the track
> Of Phoebus. Call to mind from whence we sprang:
> Ye were not form'd to live like brutes,
> But virtue to pursue and knowledge high." [22] (lines 113–117)

Cary's "knowledge high," as a rendering of Dante's single word "conoscenza," perhaps, prompted Tennyson's use of the word "knowledge" in *Ulysses* instead of the word "wisdom" which he had employed earlier for the same concept, in the formula "wisdom of the West" in *The Hesperides*. He had used the word "knowledge" with much this same connotation in an even earlier poem, *The Mystic*. Only later, as in *Locksley Hall* and in *In Memoriam*, did he obviously make a distinction between the two words, knowledge and wisdom, restricting the former to "knowledge is of things we see."

It seems fairly certain to me that Boyd's, Cary's, and Howard's translations of the Dante passage were helpful to Tennyson in re-enforcing the imagistic formula which equates the hitherto undiscovered and therefore "new" knowledge that is the goal of the oracular poet with "new worlds" far in the western sea. That the formulation was made in Tennyson's mind sometime before

---

[22] Dante: "Non vogliate negar l'esperienza,
Diretro al sol, del mondo senza gente.
"Considerate la vostra semenza:
Fatti non foste a viver come bruti,
Ma per sequir virtute e conoscenza." (lines 116–120)

Neither Boyd nor Howard approaches the force nor dignity of Cary.

Boyd: "Recall your glorious toils, your lofty birth,
Nor like the grov'ling herds, ally'd to earth,
No base despondence quit your lofty claim." (XIX, 1–3)

Howard: ". . . be resolute,
Follow the sun, and new unpeopled worlds
Explore. Cherish in mind your noble birth:
Ye were not, heroes! form'd to live like brutes,
But dare where Virtue and fair Science lead." (p. 159)

the composition of *Ulysses* seems very likely. Whether Tennyson relied on his memory or whether he had one or more of the translations actually open before him as he wrote, we have, I suppose, no secure means of ascertaining, though in my opinion the former is more likely. But it is clear that this formula is the structural device on which the poem mainly hangs. It begins its function with "I cannot rest from travel" of line 6, continues through the "arch" passage to "a bringer of new things," line 28, and to "follow knowledge like a sinking star," line 31. It is interrupted by the opposing movement of the poem, the Telemachus passage of lines 33–43, which has no overt connection with anything in Dante, Boyd, Cary, or Howard. It is operative again in Ulysses' final address to the mariners—specifically in "to seek a newer world," line 57, and in "to sail beyond the sunset, and the baths / Of all the western stars," of lines 60–61.

Boyd and Cary may also have furnished hints for line 62, which expresses the possibility of failure in the psychic journey: "It may be that the gulfs will wash us down." The "gulfs" are the instrument of destruction here. In Dante's description of the foundering of Ulysses' ships the instrument is a windstorm coming from the island mountain (of Purgatory, according to the commentators) which the ship is approaching, and the sea has only a passive function. The final line of the canto reads: "Infin che il mar fu sopra noi richiuso," which Carlyle-Wicksteed renders: ". . . til the sea was closed above us." While both Boyd and Cary continue the instrumentality of the wind, they make the waters also an instrument of the foundering. Cary's last line is: "And over us the booming billow clos'd." And Boyd's last two lines are:

> The op'ning plank receiv'd the rushing tides
> And me and mine to swift perdition sent.[23]

---

[23] Howard would seem to have given no help here:
> The demon storm,
> Thrice with the deafening billows, whirl'd us round,
> Then rais'd our shatter'd poop, and whelm'd us deep.

The active force of Cary's "booming billow" and Boyd's "rushing tides" are patently much closer than Dante's "the sea was closed over us" to Tennyson's "gulfs" that "may wash us down."

The actual destruction of Ulysses was, of course, no part of Tennyson's purpose in the poem, and the gulfs become only a very real threat of failure in the oracular poet's psychic quest. At this point Tennyson's poem, having used Dante and Boyd and Cary and Howard for all they are worth to it, takes complete leave of them. The longed-for goal of Tennyson's Ulysses, "the Happy Isles," and the hero Ulysses may see there, "the great Achilles, whom we knew," are Tennyson's; they are not Dante's.

✿✿✿

The Influence of the Traditional Ballad in Nineteenth-Century British Fiction

Ambrose N. Manning

EAST TENNESSEE STATE UNIVERSITY

In 1765 Bishop Thomas Percy published *Reliques of Ancient English Poetry*. The impact this volume of ballads had on the British poetry of the nineteenth century is well known. It seems, however, that insufficient attention has been paid to the influence which the ballad had on the nineteenth-century British novel. If such poets as Coleridge, Wordsworth, Byron, and Keats—to name only a few—used the content and/or structure of the ballad in their poetry, it seems likely that the works of their contemporaries who were writing in prose fiction would also have been influenced by the then-current interest in the ballad.

Before Bishop Percy in 1765 there had been other sources of ballads to which the nineteenth-century writers might have had access.

> The oldest deliberate collections of ballads are of broadsides. One such collection, that of Shirburn Castle, is an outstanding example. Samuel Pepys (1633–1703) became interested in ballads and built up a collection of about 2000, basing it on an earlier one by John Selden. The most important of these collections were made in the seventeenth and eighteenth centuries. John Bagford made one, almost entirely from broadside sources.[1]

Nineteenth-century authors would have had access to broadsides, even if not to the private collections.

The most important of all the early collections of ballads were

[1] MacEdward Leach, *The Ballad Book* (New York, 1955), p. 34.

those of Bishop Percy and Sir Walter Scott. Other collections were made and published by Allan Ramsey (1724), David Herd (1769), Joseph Ritson (1787–1795), Robert Jamieson (1806), and George Kinloch (1827).

The serious study of folk songs and ballads, then, began in the eighteenth century and was extended into the nineteenth. The interest in the ballad rather obviously affected the literature of the nineteenth century. "The romantic period in literature undoubtedly stimulated ballad scholarship also." [2]

A good place to begin examining the influence of ballads on nineteenth-century fiction, it seems to me, is with an author who was involved in the collection of ballads, who wrote poetry, and who was both a good and a prolific novelist of the early nineteenth century—Sir Walter Scott.

Scott's interest in old songs and lore in general led him to organize a corps of helpers who contributed much traditional material to his collection. As Bishop Percy did, he often changed an original or inserted lost stanzas. But the *Minstrelsy of the Scottish Border*, published in 1802, remains one of our most valuable sources of ballads. "Scott's enthusiasm and his wide knowledge of folklore and history made his collection and comments of great critical worth." [3]

After the publication of his *Minstrelsy* and after his success as a poet, Scott turned to the novel. Because of his interest in the history and traditions of Scotland and England, many of his novels are based on factual incidents in these two countries. In 1818 he published *Rob Roy*, a novel which has as its source the ballad of the same name relating the exploits of a Scottish Robin Hood.

In the "Appendices To Introduction" of *Rob Roy*, Scott says:

> The achievement of Robert Oig, or Young Rob Roy, as the Lowlanders called him, was celebrated in a ballad, of which there are twenty different and various editions. The tune is

[2] Kenneth and Mary Clarke, *Introducing Folklore* (New York, 1963), p. 10.
[3] Leach, p. 35.

30

lively and wild, and we select the following words from memory:

> Rob Roy is frae the Hielands come,
>   Down to the Lawland border;
> And he has stolen that lady away,
>   To hand his house in order.
>
> He set her on a milk-white steed,
>   Of none he stood in awe;
> Untill they reached the Hieland hills,
>   Aboon the Balmaha'!
>
> Saying, "Be content, be content,
>   Be content with me, Lady;
> Where will ye find in Lennox land,
>   Sae braw a man as me, Lady?
>
> "Rob Roy, he was my father called,
>   Mac Gregor was his name, Lady;
> A' the country, far and near,
>   Have heard Mac Gregor's fame, Lady.
>
> "He was a hedge about his friends,
>   A heckle to his foes, Lady;
> If any man did him gainsay,
>   He felt his deadly blows, Lady.
>
> "I am as bold, I am as bold,
>   I am as bold and more, Lady;
> Ony man that doubts my work,
>   May try my gude claymore, Lady.
>
> "Then be content, be content,
>   Be content with me, Lady;
> For now you are my wedded wife,
>   Until the day ye die, Lady." [4]

In *Rob Roy*, Scott frequently quotes passages from old songs and ballads; and as in many of his other novels, he uses as chapter tags and mottoes stanzas from ballads. For example, as an intro-

---

[4] *The Waverly Novels, Vol. IV: Rob Roy* (New York, n.d.), pp. 498–499. Subsequent references are to this edition.

duction to Chapter 11 he cites a verse from an "old Scotch Ballad" which is as follows:

> What gars ye gaunt, my merymen a'?
> What gars ye look so dreary?
> What gars ye hing your head sae sair
> In the castle of Balwearie? (p. 171)

Chapters 14 and 23 are also introduced by excerpts from ballads and old songs.

To cite an instance of the employment of the ballad within the text of this novel: in Chapter 18 Scott has Andrew, the smuggler, serving as a guide to Rob Roy.

> The pale beams of the morning were now enlightening the horizon when Andrew cast a look behind him, and, not seeing the appearance of a living being on the moors which he had travelled, his hard features gradually unbent, as he first whistled, then sung with much glee and little melody, the end of one of his native songs:
>
> > "Jenny, lass! I think I hae her
> > Ower the moor amang the heather;
> > All their clan shall never get her." (p. 247)

Chapter 29 of *Rob Roy* includes a stanza of one of the Robin Hood ballads.

The same year in which he published *Roy Roy* Scott wrote another novel with a Scottish setting, *The Heart of Midlothian*. As one might expect there are several snatches of ballads and folk songs in this novel also. No fewer than five chapters are introduced by quotes from ballads, one of which, at the beginning of Chapter 17, is a stanza from the familiar "Ballad of Little Musgrave":

> And some they whistled—and some they sang,
> And so me did loudly say,
> Whenever Lord Barnard's horn it blew,
> "Away, Musgrave, away!" [5]

[5] *The Waverly Novels, Volume VI: The Heart of Midlothian* (New York, n.d.), p. 200. Subsequent references are to this edition.

In Chapter 10 of this novel Effie and Jeanie Deans are discussing Effie's secret lover. If Effie would name her seducer, the penalty for her moral offense would not be severe. Effie's indiscretion with all its consequences and repercussions and Jeanie's effort to help her are the essential elements of the plot and theme of *The Heart of Midlothian*. Scott writes of Effie:

> She looked at her [Jeanie] with a sly air, in which there was something like irony, as she chanted, in a low but marked tone, a scrap of an old Scotch song.
>
> "Through the kirkyard
> I met wi' the Laird,
> The silly puir body he said me nae harm;
> But just ere 'twas dark,
> I met wi' the clerk—" (p. 120)

This fragment of the ballad accurately reflects Effie's experience. Five chapters later Scott writes:

> A voice was heard to sing one of those wild and monotonous strains so common in Scotland, and to which the natives of that country chant their old ballads. . . . When the sounds were renewed, the words were distinctly audible:
>
> "When the glede's in the blue cloud,
> The lavrock lies still;
> When the hound's in the green-wood,
> The hind keeps the hill." (p. 188)

And in Chapter 17:

> He [Ratcliffe] then began to hum, but in a very low and suppressed tone, the first stanza of a favourite ballad of Wildfire's . . . :
>
> "There's a bloodhound ranging Tinwald wood,
> There's harness glancing sheen;
> There's a maiden sits on Tinwald brae,
> And she sings loud between."

Madge [Wildfire] had no sooner received the catch-word, than she vindicated Ratcliffe's sagacity by setting off at score with the song:

"O sleep ye sound, Sir James, she said,
    When ye suld rise and ride?
There's twenty men, wi' bow and blade,
    Are seeking where ye hide." (pp. 210–211)

Occasionally Scott comments directly on the correspondence of a ballad and the mood or theme of a novel. In Chapter 40 when Madge Murdockson—or Wildfire—is dying, Scott says:

And it was remarkable, that there could always be traced in her songs something appropriate, though perhaps only obliquely or collaterally so, to her present situation. Her next seemed to be the fragment of some ballad:

"Cauld is my bed, Lord Archibald,
    And sad my sleep of sorrow;
But thine sall be as sad and cauld,
    My fause true-love! to-morrow.

And weep ye not, my maidens free,
    Though death your mistress borrow;
For he for whom I die to-day,
    Shall die for me to-morrow." (p. 471)

She follows that song with another ballad on the theme of Proud Maisie and Sweet Robin.

Many other examples in which ballads are mentioned or passages from ballads are quoted appear in *The Heart of Midlothian* as well as others of Scott's novels. Because Scott is usually considered a highly romantic author, one might expect him to reflect his interest in the ballad in his prose works. Scott, however, was not necessarily representative of the British prose fiction writer of the nineteenth century. But what about Charles Dickens?

Of all the nineteenth-century British novelists, Dickens would probably be considered the least likely to make references to the ballad in his fiction. Yet in Chapter 26 of *Oliver Twist* there is a scene in which this type of folk song is mentioned. When Fagin is looking for Monks, he goes into the public-house, The Three Cripples, or Cripples. Dickens writes: "As Fagin stepped softly

34

in, the professional gentleman, running over the keys by way of prelude, occasioned a general cry of order for a song; which having subsided, a young lady proceeded to entertain the company with a ballad in four verses." [6]

Another novel in which Dickens refers to the ballad is *Our Mutual Friend*. In this case the ballad is probably not the traditional folk song but the broadsides of which Silas Wegg has copies in his street stall where Mr. Boffin first discovers him. In Chapter 5 of the First Book of this novel Silas addresses Mr. Boffin:

On which occasion, as the ballad that was made about it ["Decline and Fall of The Rooshan Empire"] describes.

"Beside that cottage door . . . ,
A girl was on her knees;
She held aloft a snowy scarf . . . ,
Which . . . fluttered in the breeze." [7]

Then in Chapter 6 of the Third Book of the same novel Dickens has this passage:

"Brothers in arms," said Mr. Wegg, in excellent spirits, "welcome!" In return, Mr. Venus gave him a rather dry goodevening. "Walk in, brother," said Silas, clapping him on the shoulder, "and take your seat in my chimney corner; for what says the ballad?

'No malice to dread, sir,
And no false hood to fear . . . .'" (p. 483)

Charles Dickens wrote a novel in collaboration with Wilkie Collins in Paris during the winter of 1855–56 entitled *The Wreck of the Golden Mary*. Almost all of Chapter 28 of this novel is a 28-stanza poem which the authors introduce with this comment: "An old seaman in the Surf-boat sang this ballad, as his story, to a curious sort of tuneful no-tune." [8] The subject of

[6] New York, n.d., p. 195.
[7] New York, n.d., p. 60. Subsequent reference is to this edition.
[8] New York, 1956, p. 112.

this ballad is a ship wreck and is appropriate for this novel, the plot of which revolves around a ship wreck.

And of course near the first of Dickens' famous *A Christmas Carol* there are the familiar lines of the folk Christmas carol:

> "God bless you, merry gentlemen!
> May nothing you dismay." [9]

There are undoubtedly references to ballads in some of the others of Dickens' novels, but these which have been pointed out are sufficient to show that this famous nineteenth-century novelist was aware of the ballad as a popular medium of oral communication and employed this folk-art form in his fiction.

William Makepeace Thackeray apparently disregards the ballad in his major fiction; there is, however, at least one reference to the ballad in his essays. The essays entitled *The Fitz-Boodle Papers* (George Fitz-Boodle, Esquire to Oliver Yorke, Esquire) include the section Thackeray labeled "Fitz-Boodle," in which he cites two so-called German ballads: "The Willow Tree," which has seven verses of eight lines each, and "Fairy Days," which has six stanzas of six lines each. [10]

One might expect to find ballads and references to the ballad in the novels of the Brontë sisters, for they read and admired the British Romantic poets, and they had music lessons in which they might have been exposed to some of the traditional tunes and lyrics. And the expectation is verified in *Wuthering Heights* when Emily Brontë in Chapter 23 has Linton, the young, frail sickly son of Heathcliff, saying to the young, comforting Catherine:

> "Sit on the settle and let me lean on your knee. That's as mama used to do, whole afternoons together. Sit quite still and don't talk: but you may sing a song, if you can sing; or you may say a nice long interesting ballad—one of those you promised to teach me: or a story. I'd rather have a ballad, though: begin."

[9] *A Christmas Carol, Christmas Tales* (New York, 1947), p. 21.
[10] *Burlesques, Part II* (Boston, 1889), pp. 184–185.

36

Catherine repeated the longest she could remember. The employment pleased both mightily. Linton would have another; and after that another.[11]

Catherine and Linton are forcibly married, and Linton dies. By this time Catherine is interested in Hareton, and she teaches him to read. Chapter 31 includes the scene in which Catherine becomes exasperated with Hareton, who is beginning to realize that he loves her, because his favorite literature happens to be hers; and she feels that he is profaning the selections she recalls with nostalgia. Hareton angrily leaves the room and presently returns with a half dozen volumes in his hands. He throws the books into Catherine's lap: "She opened one that had obviously been often turned over, and read a portion in the drawling tone of a beginner; then laughed, and threw it from her. 'And listen,' she continued provokingly, commencing a verse of an old ballad in the same fashion" (p. 315).

As indicated above, Emily Brontë refers to the ballad in her well-known novel *Wuthering Heights;* so does her sister Charlotte in the equally famous novel *Jane Eyre.* At the beginning of the story, Jane is living with the Reed family, but feels discriminated against. On this evening as the three Reed children are gathered around their mother, Jane retires to a window-seat with a book which she has slipped from the bookcase in the drawing-room. Charlotte Brontë describes Jane's reading: "Each picture told a story; mysterious often to my undeveloped understanding and imperfect feelings, yet ever profoundly interesting: as interesting as the tales Bessie sometimes narrated on winter evenings, when she chanced to be in good humour; and when, having brought her ironing-table to the nursery-hearth, she allowed us to sit about it, and while she got up Mrs. Reed's lace frills, and crimped her nightcap borders, fed our eager attention with passages of love and adventure taken from old fairy tales and older ballads." [12]

---

[11] New York, 1907, p. 251. Subsequent reference is to this edition.
[12] New York, 1944, p. 5. Subsequent reference is to this edition.

A couple of chapters later Bessie, after completing her chores, begins making a new bonnet for Georgiana's doll—

Meantime she sang: her song was

> "In the days when we went gipsying,
> A long time ago."

I had often heard the song before, and always with lively delight; for Bessie had a sweet voice,—at least, I thought so. But now, though her voice was still sweet, I found in its melody an indescribable sadness. Sometimes, preoccupied with her work, she sang the refrain very low, very lingeringly: "a long time ago" came out like the saddest cadence of a funeral hymn. She passed into another ballad, this time a really doleful one. (p. 19)

The ballad Bessie sings is a five-stanza ballad about a poor orphan child.

Another British novelist who appears to have been influenced by the ballad is George Eliot. There is no specific reference to the ballad in *Adam Bede;* however, there are, according to one scholar, many parallels between Hetty Sorrel and the Forlorn Maiden of the traditional ballad:

> In the first place, each woman kills her baby. . . . Secondly, each mother is incapable of looking at the babe and remaining resolute. . . . Thirdly, each mother buries her baby and at the same location, by a tree. . . . A fourth point of parallel is that each mother reaches a state of complete despair. And finally, each tale includes a reference to the supernatural.[13]

These parallels along with direct allusions to the *Lyrical Ballads,* in which Wordsworth employs the theme, make it probable that the similarity between Hetty and the conventional Forlorn Maiden is not simply coincidental or subconscious, but deliberate.

One obvious instance in which George Eliot makes use of the ballad occurs in *Middlemarch.* The chapter tag for Chapter 84

[13] Thomas G. Burton, "Hetty Sorrel, the Forlorn Maiden," *The Victorian Newsletter,* No. 30 (Fall 1966), p. 25.

38

of this piece of fiction is a stanza of the ballad "The Nut-Brown Maid"—or as she spells it "Not-browne Mayde." [14]

One of the authors of the late nineteenth century who makes frequent references to the ballad, although certainly not a Romantic as some of his immediate predecessors were, is Thomas Hardy. It is generally recognized that Hardy includes several aspects of folklore in his writing: folk speech, proverbs, beliefs and superstitions, holidays and celebrations, games, and customs. He also makes frequent references to the folk songs and ballads of the Wessex country.

In an article on the traditional basis of Hardy's fiction, Donald Davidson states: "The characteristic Hardy novel is conceived as a *told* (or *sung*) story, or at least not as a literary story; . . . it is an extension in the form of a modern prose fiction, of a traditional ballad or an oral tale." [15] He then proceeds to show how Hardy's stories resemble the traditional narrative. In regard to Hardy's characters, Davidson says: "They have the changelessness of the figures of traditional narrative from epic, saga, and romance to broadside balladry and its prose parallels." [16] Davidson's thesis is that Hardy is so much a product of his environment—Wessex—that his fiction reflects the traditional narrative in structure, theme, and character portrayal. Hardy also makes specific reference to ballads in some of his novels.

Hardy's first successful novel was *Far from the Madding Crowd,* published in 1874. It is this novel in which Hardy establishes the theme which he uses quite frequently in his other novels: the contrast of a patient and generous devotion—in this case the shepherd, Gabriel Oak—with a selfish, unscrupulous love and violent passion—in this novel, Bathsheba Everdene. It is in Chapter 23 that Bathsheba says to Joseph Poorgrass after a shearing-supper:

[14] *The Works of George Eliot, Vol. VI: Middlemarch* (New York, n.d.), p. 816.

[15] "The Traditional Basis of Thomas Hardy's Fiction," *Still Rebels, Still Yankees and Other Essays* (Baton Rouge, 1957), p. 49.

[16] Davidson, p. 56.

"Now, Joseph, your song, please. . . ."

"Well, really, ma'am," he replied in a yielding tone, "I don't know what to say. It would be a poor plain ballet of my own composure."

"Hear, hear!" said the supper-party.

Poorgrass, thus assured, trilled forth a flickering yet commendable piece of sentiment, the tune which consisted of the key-note and another, the latter being the sound chiefly dwelt upon. This was so successful that he rashly plunged into a second in the same breath, after a few false starts:

> I sow'-ed th'e . . . .
> I sow'-ed . . . .
> I sow'-ed the'e seeds' of' love',
>   I-it was' all' i' in the'e spring',
>   I-in A'pril', Ma'-ay, a'-nd sun'-ny' June',
> When sma'-all Bi'irds they' do' sing.

"Go on, Joseph—go on . . . ," said Coggan. "Tis a very catching ballet. Now then again—the next bar; I'll help ye to flourish up the shrill notes where yer wind is rather wheezy:

> O the wi'-il-lo'-ow tree' will' twist',
> And the wil'-low' tre'-ee wi'-ill twine."

Jacob Smallbury . . . volunteered a ballad as inclusive and interminable as that which the worthy toper old Silenus amused on a similar occasion the swains Chromis and Mnasylus, and other jolly dogs of his day.[17]

Then on the next page of this novel there is a reference to a passage from one of the ballads in Francis J. Child's *The English and Scottish Popular Ballads,* a ballad which originally comes from Scott's *Minstrelsy of the Scottish Border.*

Hardy continues: "Next came the question of the evening. Would Miss Everdene sing to them the song she always sang so charmingly—'The Banks of Allan Water'—before they went home?" (p. 178). To Gabriel Oak's flute accompaniment she sang the ballad:

[17] New York, 1918, pp. 176–177. Subsequent references are to this edition.

For his bride a soldier sought her,
And a winning tongue had he:
On the banks of Allan Water
None was gay as she. (p. 179)

Four years after *Far from the Madding Crowd* was published, Hardy produced another great work, *The Return of the Native*. In Chapter Three Hardy writes of Granfer Cantle:

With his stick in his hand, he began to jig a private minuet . . . also began to sing, in the voice of a bee up a flue:—

"The king' call'd down his no'-bles all',
By one', by two', by three';
Earl Mar'-shal, I'll' go shrive' the queen',
And thou' shalt wend' with me'." [18]

Francis B. Gummere recognizes Hardy's accuracy in portraying the Wessex peasant:

Mr. Thomas Hardy is good authority for the ways of the Wessex peasant; and the aged Wessex peasant of forty years ago, when he sang a ballad, had four centuries of the habit behind him. There is much to be learned from Granfer Cantle's eccentric performance on Blackbarrow . . . ; the "sing," the "say," and something of choral reminiscence are all there. [19]

In 1886 Hardy published his next significant novel, *The Mayor of Casterbridge*. As in *Far from the Madding Crowd* he quotes an excerpt from a ballad which Francis J. Child calls "Allan Water" or "Annan Water," and which Child credits to Sir Walter Scott. Interestingly, in his earlier novel Hardy called this ballad, which relates the story of a lover who is drowned on his way to visit his mistress, "The Banks of Allan Water." In Chapter Eight of *The Mayor of Casterbridge* Farfrae, the Scotsman, sings to an enraptured audience "Annan Water," six lines of which Hardy cites.

Also in Chapter Eight, four or five pages after the reference to "Annan Water," Hardy writes that Farfrae

[18] New York, 1912, p. 20.
[19] *The Popular Ballad* (New York, 1959), p. 248.

softly tuned an old ditty that she [Elizabeth-Jane] seemed to suggest—

> "As I came in by my bower door,
>   As day was waxin' wearie,
> Oh wha came tripping down the stair
>   But bonnie Peg my dearie." [20]

All the fragments of ballads which Hardy uses in this novel are sung by Farfrae. For example, in Chapter 27 when Elizabeth-Jane and Lucetta visit the new seed-drill which Farfrae has purchased, the one-time friend and now enemy of Henchard is humming "The Lass of Gourie."

There are at least another couple of references to the old songs and ballads which Farfrae recalls.

Near the end of the century—1891, to be exact—Hardy completed another masterpiece, *Tess of the D'Urbervilles*. When Tess returns from the man who has seduced her and does not fulfill his promise to marry her, she is despondent for some time. In Chapter 13 there is the following paragraph: "In the course of a few weeks Tess revived sufficiently to show herself so far as was necessary to get to church one Sunday morning. She liked to hear the chanting—such as it was—and the old Psalms, and to join in the Morning Hymn. That innate love of melody, which she had inherited from her ballad-singing mother, gave the simplest music a power over her which could well-nigh drag her heart out of her bosom at times." [21]

Later Tess recalls a specific song she learned from her mother. In Chapter 32 when she is preparing for her wedding, Hardy writes as follows:

> Alone, she stood for a moment before the glass looking at the effect of her silk attire; and then there came into her head her mother's ballad of the mystic robe—
>
> > That never would become that wife
> > That had once done amiss,

[20] New York, 1959, p. 57.
[21] New York, 1920, p. 106. Subsequent references are to this edition.

which Mrs. Durbeyfield had used to sing to her as a child. (p. 263)

Near the end of the novel (Chapter 49) Hardy writes:

> Sighs were expended on the wish that she had taken more notice of the tunes he played on his harp, that she had inquired more curiously of him which were his favourite ballads among those the country girls sang. She indirectly inquired of Amby Seedling . . . , and by chance Amby remembered that, amongst the snatches of melody in which they had indulged at the dairyman's, to induce the cows to let down their milk, Clare had seemed to like "Cupid's Gardens," "I have parks, I have hounds," and "The break o' the day"; and had seemed not to care for "The Tailor's Breeches," and "Such a Beauty did I grow," excellent ditties as they were.
>
> To perfect the ballads was now her whimsical desire. She practised them privately at odd moments, especially "The break o' the day":
>
> > Arise, arise, arise!
> > And pick your love a posy,
> > All o' the sweetest flowers
> > That in the garden grow.
> > The turtle doves and sma' birds
> > In every bough a-building,
> > So early in the May-time,
> > At the break o' the day! (p. 436)

Hardy also refers to a ballad in at least one other novel. In Chapter 20 of *The Woodlanders* he mentions "a local ballad— 'O come in from the foggy, foggy dew.' "[22]

Briefly, to name another couple of nineteenth-century British novelists who reflect some familiarity with the ballad in their fiction, there are Anthony Trollope and George Meredith.

Near the middle of the nineteenth century, 1857, Trollope wrote his famous *Barchester Towers*. Chapter 27 has a couple of lines from a song of which a whole stanza is cited in Chapter 46. In both cases the excerpt is given in the context of Mr. Slope's

[22] New York, 1958, p. 177.

giving advice. The verse that is rendered in the latter chapter is as follows:

> It's gude to be merry and wise, Mr. Slope;
> It's gude to be honest and true;
> It's gude to be off with the old love—Mr. Slope,
> Before you are on with the new.[23]

Earlier in Chapter 27, of course, "Mr. Slope" had been left off at the ends of lines one and three. There was more dialect, too. In fact, the couplet was rendered:

> "It's gude to be off with the auld luve
> Before ye be on wi' the new." (p. 247)

Even George Meredith as late as 1895 in his novel *The Amazing Marriage* makes at least a passing reference to the ballad. In Chapter 34 Meredith makes the statement that ballads grow "like mushrooms from a scuffle of feet on grass overnight." [24]

The conclusion from this study, then, is that all the major British writers of prose fiction in the nineteenth century made some use of the ballad, some more extensively than others, naturally. Beginning with Sir Walter Scott, who collected ballads himself and might be expected to use them in his novels and who wrote at the height of the Romantic period, early in the century, and ending with Thomas Hardy and George Meredith, who were writing at the end of the century, we have a total of nine major novelists who in one way or another—thematically, through character portrayal, or through parallel of plots—were influenced significantly by the traditional ballad.

[23] New York, 1945, p. 456. Subsequent reference is to this edition.
[24] Quoted in Gummere, p. 14.

The Three Faces of Hamlet

Bain Tate Stewart

THE UNIVERSITY OF TENNESSEE

Students of *Hamlet* may recall with profit the words written some thirty years ago by Dr. S. I. Hayakawa in *Language in Action.* "Cow$_1$," wrote Dr. Hayakawa, "Is Not Cow$_2$." Considered in one sense this statement implies that there may be many Hamlets, as there are many readers and viewers of Shakespeare's play. Another suggestion of Dr. Hayakawa's words—one nearer to his intended meaning—is that the bitterly disillusioned Hamlet whom we meet for the first time in the second scene of the play is not the brilliant young courtier who existed before the play began and who is remembered and admired by Ophelia; nor is he yet the antic Hamlet he is soon to become, nor the poised fatalist of Act V. During the action of the play, Shakespeare's Hamlet shows, in fact, three faces, similar yet different, three appearances behind which the inner reality of his character must be sought; and unless we distinguish these appearances clearly, the reality may escape us altogether.

Hamlet$_1$, as he appears on stage in Scene 2, concealing beneath his "inky cloak" his profound disillusionment and frustration, is, of course, very different in both appearance and reality from the young prince whom we would have observed two months earlier before his father's death or even one month earlier before his mother's remarriage. The clearest, most explicit indication of what Hamlet once was is contained in the words of Ophelia, just after Hamlet has repudiated their former relationship, denounced her and her sex, and ordered her to a nunnery:

O, what a noble mind is here o'er-thrown!
The courtier's, soldier's, scholar's, eye, tongue, sword;
The expectancy and rose of the fair state,
The glass of fashion and the mould of form,
The observed of all observers, quite, quite down!
And I, of ladies most deject and wretched,
That suck'd the honey of his music vows,
Now see that noble and most sovereign reason,
Like sweet bells jangled, out of tune and harsh;
That unmatch'd form and feature of blown youth
Blasted with ecstasy: O, woe is me,
To have seen what I have seen, see what I see!

(III. i. 158–169) [1]

The ideal of youthful nobility and courtesy suggested by Ophelia's words is occasionally reflected in Hamlet's behavior early in the play, especially when he is greeting old friends and acquaintances: Horatio (I. ii. 160 ff.), for example, or the players (II. ii. 440 ff.) or even Rosencrantz and Guildenstern (II. ii. 226 ff.) before he discovers their mission. Hamlet's whole relationship with Horatio, moreover, reveals a great deal about his basic nature. His first words of greeting, "Horatio,—or I do forget myself," suggest the identity of natures which, to the Elizabethans, was the distinguishing feature of true friendship. In a sense, then, when we observe Horatio, we observe what Hamlet has been and what he might have remained under other circumstances. And in Hamlet's words to and about Horatio, we recognize a reflection of Hamlet's own nature:

Since my dear soul was mistress of her choice
And could of men distinguish her election,
S'hath seal'd thee for herself; for thou hast been
As one, in suffering all, that suffers nothing,
A man that fortune's buffets and rewards
Hast ta'en with equal thanks: and blest are those
Whose blood and judgement are so well commeddled,
That they are not a pipe for fortune's finger

---

[1] Citations are to *The Complete Works of Shakespeare*, ed. Hardin Craig (New York, 1951).

To sound what stop she please. Give me that man
That is not passion's slave, and I will wear him
In my heart's core, ay, in my heart of heart,
As I do thee. (III. ii. 68–79)

Clearly Hamlet, if he is similar to his friend, is not by nature a man who may properly be described as "passion's slave." The state in which we see him at the beginning of the play could only have been brought about by some profound emotional involvement, and Shakespeare takes pains to remind us that a significant change has taken place in Hamlet during the two months between his father's death and the beginning of the play.

From the beginning of the play each face which Hamlet reveals to the audience is consistently hidden or disguised from even his closest associates (with the occasional exception of Horatio) behind a carefully contrived mask—at first of grief, later of madness. When Hamlet appears for the first time upon the stage, there is surely irony as well as plain truth in his answer to Gertrude's question as to why his father's death "seems . . . so particular" to him: "Seems, madam! Nay, it is; I know not 'seems' . . . . / But I have that within which passeth show; / These but the trappings and the suits of woe" (I. ii. 76, 85–86). From his first moment upon the stage Hamlet is a seemer, a pretender. Before Gertrude and Claudius and the other members of the court, he carefully maintains the fiction that his melancholy and dejection are caused by the death of his father. But a few moments later when, alone, he speaks plainly, without simulation and from the heart, the elder Hamlet is remembered with respect and admiration rather than with excessive grief; and Hamlet's bitter disillusionment with the "unweeded garden" of this world reflects not despair at the realization of mortality but disgust with the grossness and sensuality of his mother's behavior:

But two months dead: Nay, not so much, not two:
So excellent a king; that was, to this,
Hyperion to a satyr; so loving to my mother

That he might not beteem the winds of heaven
Visit her face too roughly. Heaven and earth!
Must I remember? Why, she would hang on him,
As if increase of appetite had grown
By what it fed on: and yet, within a month—
Let me not think on't—Frailty, thy name is woman! . . .
    O, most wicked speed, to post
With such dexterity to incestuous sheets!
It is not nor it cannot come to good:
But break, my heart, for I must hold my tongue.
                              (I. ii. 138–159)

The last line of this passage carries a special significance. As
Hamlet sees it, the ultimate cause of his heartbreak is the neces-
sity to remember and be silent. If he could speak—to Gertrude—
the bitter thoughts which he has poured out here in solitude,
he might again find meaning in life. The attitudes so plainly
suggested in this soliloquy—disgust with his mother's sensuality,
affectionate remembrance of his father's greatness—are repeated
in the immediately following conversation between Hamlet and
Horatio as Hamlet expresses to Horatio his revulsion at the
wedding which "followed hard upon" his father's funeral—
"Would I had met my dearest foe in heaven / Or ever I had seen
that day, Horatio!" (I. ii. 182–183)—and then pays tribute to
his father in words which express the essence of manly grief and
restraint: "He was a man, take him for all in all, / I shall not look
upon his like again" (I. ii. 188–189).

If Hamlet remained throughout the play as he has clearly
appeared to the audience in the early scenes, there would be no
Hamlet problem. With the delivery of the ghost's message, however, Hamlet assumes, with his "antic disposition," a second face,
or appearance to the audience, which is as variable and clouded
as the first had been constant and plain. This is the Hamlet—as
he appears from the last scene of Act I, when the ghost pronounces to him its injunction to revenge, through the passionate,
private interview with Gertrude at the end of Act III—who,
uncertain and indecisive, seems to defy explanation or understanding and who leaves us with questions for which the answers

never seem to be altogether satisfying. Is he, in fact, mad or merely pretending to be mad for his own purposes and perhaps at times for his pleasure? What is his real attitude toward death? Does he trust the ghost? What has been his relationship with Ophelia, and what are his feelings toward her? Why, after promising to sweep to his revenge "with wings as swift / As meditation or the thoughts of love" (I. v. 29–30), does he so shortly declare, "The time is out of joint: O cursed spite, / That ever I was born to set it right!" (I. v. 189–190)? And why does he delay, for weeks and months, until seemingly he accomplishes his revenge only because of the ineptitude with which Claudius and Laertes carry out their plot against his life? Clearly Hamlet himself cannot answer these questions for us, for he no longer fully understands himself. The great meditative soliloquies in the last scene of the second act and the first scene of the third pose more problems than they resolve.

We shall remain upon the safe way to an understanding of the fullness of Hamlet's character if we recognize that while much of mystery and complexity has been added in this second face which he reveals to the audience, little of consequence has been taken away. Even after the discovery of his father's murder, the moral degradation of his mother continues to be a principal cause for his distress. The ghost concludes the long account of the murder with explicit directions for Hamlet's future conduct toward both Claudius and Gertrude:

> If thou hast nature in thee, bear it not;
> Let not the royal bed of Denmark be
> A couch for luxury and damned incest.
> But, howsoever thou pursuest this act,
> Taint not thy mind, nor let thy soul contrive
> Against thy mother aught: leave her to heaven
> And to those thorns that in her bosom lodge,
> To prick and sting her. (I. v. 81–88)

And to the ghost's parting words, "Hamlet, remember me," Hamlet replies, after a dozen lines of impassioned invocation and hyperbole, "Yes, by heaven! / O most pernicious woman! / O villain, villain, smiling damned villain!" (I. v. 104–106). It is significant that, after listening to the ghost's detailed account of Claudius's villainy, Hamlet's first reference is to Gertrude rather than to Claudius. Of the two injunctions which the ghost has laid upon him, the second, "Leave her to heaven" and to her own conscience, is as great a burden as the first. One reason, it seems, that Hamlet cannot bring himself to plan and carry out retribution against Claudius is that his whole nature demands first some settlement with Gertrude.

Throughout the second and third acts, Hamlet's passionate need to come to terms with Gertrude—a need which is both forbidden by the admonition of his father's ghost and thwarted by circumstances—is perhaps suggested in his ambivalent relationship with Ophelia, who now attracts and repels him as Gertrude does. And some of his wild words spoken to Ophelia (and perhaps intended also for the listening ears of Polonius) take on added point and significance if they are thought of as addressed in imagination to Gertrude, his prototype of fallen womanhood:

> If thou dost marry, I'll give thee this plague
> for thy dowry: be thou as chaste as ice,
> as pure as snow, thou shalt not escape
> calumny. Get thee to a nunnery, go:
> farewell. Or, if thou wilt needs marry,
> marry a fool; for wise men know well
> enough what monsters you make of them . . . .
> I have heard of your paintings too, well
> enough; God has given you one face,
> and you make yourselves another: you
> jig, you amble, and you lisp, and nick-name
> God's creatures, and make your wantonness
> your ignorance. Go to, I'll no more on't;
> it hath made me mad. I say, we will
> have no more marriages: those that are
> married already, all but one, shall live;
> the rest shall keep as they are.
> To a nunnery, go. (III. i. 138–157)

Almost nothing in Ophelia's nature or behavior makes these lines especially applicable to her, but the passage mirrors with considerable insight the conduct of an older woman attempting to make herself attractive to a new husband.

Another indication of Hamlet's continuing obsession with his mother's behavior is given immediately after the revelation of Claudius's unmistakable guilt during the play within the play. As an immediate effect of his discovery Hamlet is freed to speak openly and directly to his mother, but he is not yet able to take decisive action against Claudius. In the brief soliloquy which ends the mouse-trap scene, Hamlet's references to both words and actions concern only his mother:

> Soft! now to my mother.
> O heart, lose not thy nature; let not ever
> The soul of Nero enter this firm bosom:
> Let me be cruel, not unnatural:
> I will speak daggers to her but use none.
> (III. ii. 410–414)

And among the many explanations which have been advanced for Hamlet's refusal to kill Claudius when the kneeling king is wholly within his power, we may properly emphasize the possibility that Hamlet simply does not wish to be diverted from, and perhaps denied, the confrontation with his mother to which he is bound and which has been his most insistent desire since the beginning of the play.

Like Hamlet's encounter with the ghost in Act I, his confrontation with Gertrude at the end of Act III marks a distinct change in his basic attitude and behavior. In this scene he experiences for the first time the release of tension and the understanding and acceptance of his destined role which characterize the last of his three faces as we have distinguished them in the play. The principal cause of this final change seems to be the free expression to Gertrude of the suspicions and recriminations which Hamlet has repressed for months within himself, combined perhaps with the earlier resolution, during the mouse-trap scene, of any doubts which he may truly have held concerning the honesty of the ghost. Whatever the causes, the change is sudden and apparent.

The Hamlet of the last two acts differs from his earlier self principally in his changed concept of the individual's moral responsibility and the power of the individual man to alter the world in which he lives. At the beginning of the play Hamlet is disgusted by his mother's violation of his own standards of morality; after the ghost's revelation and throughout most of Acts II and III, he is distressed and dismayed also by the responsibility for revenge which has been forced upon him. After the precipitous killing of Polonius in his mother's private chamber, however, he seizes upon a thought which will guide his future actions, the thought that it is, after all, God's will, not man's, that will be done:

> For this same lord,
> I do repent: but heaven hath pleased it so,
> To punish me with this and this with me,
> That I must be their scourge and minister.
> (III. iv. 172–175)

And later he concludes that his escape, through "rashness" and indiscretion, from the death commissioned for him in England "should teach us / There's a divinity that shapes our ends, / Rough-hew them how we will" (V. ii. 9–11). Thus lessoned, he can calmly dismiss his own premonition of death and Horatio's warning just before the fencing match with Laertes: "Not a whit, we defy augury: there's a special providence in the fall of a sparrow. If it be now, 'tis not to come; if it be not to come, it will be now; if it be not now, yet it will come: the readiness is all" (V. ii. 230–234).

In the last acts of the play there is only one brief scene which suggests the continuation of Hamlet's disturbed and uncertain questioning beyond the confrontation with Gertrude. As he is leaving Denmark for England, Hamlet pauses for a moment to observe Fortinbras and his soldiers marching "to gain a little patch of ground / That hath in it no profit but the name" (IV. iv. 18–19). The sight provokes once more Hamlet's efforts to explain the reasons for his delayed revenge, and he concludes: "I do not know / Why yet I live to say 'This thing 's to do;' / Sith I have cause and will and strength and means / To do't" (IV. iv. 43–46). The mood and tone of this soliloquy are more appropriate, however, for our second Hamlet than for the third. Perhaps they are spoken here as a reminder of his earlier state of mind. Or perhaps, as *Hamlet* took final form in Shakespeare's mind as he observed its performance upon the stage of the Globe Theatre, he came to recognize that the passage, compelling though it is as poetry, is dramatically superfluous at this point in the play. The First Folio eliminates the soliloquy altogether.

Throughout the fourth and fifth acts Hamlet continues, of course, to use the convenient mask of his antic disposition—in his conversation with Rosencrantz and Guildenstern near the beginning of Act IV, for example, in the following meeting with Claudius, and perhaps later at the grave of Ophelia. Throughout the last scenes of the play, however, Hamlet frequently makes no real effort to conceal from his companions the face which he clearly reveals to the audience. This relative openness of manner is an indication of Hamlet's new poise and confidence.

By recognizing, in an echo of Dr. Hayakawa's words, that Hamlet$_1$ is not Hamlet$_2$ and Hamlet$_2$ is not Hamlet$_3$, we may make a significant and helpful modification in our approach to the understanding of Hamlet; for we are able to accept partial and tentative rather than absolute answers to the questions about his nature and behavior which demand our attention. We will not expect to find the same degree of love or hate reflected in his conduct at every moment in the play, and we will not be surprised by the change from his callous treatment of Ophelia just before the play within the play to the genuine grief and remorse which he expresses at her burial. We will not expect any single explanation for Hamlet's delay to apply with equal validity to the disturbed, bitter, uncertain Hamlet of Acts II and III and to the relatively poised and understanding, though still melancholy, Hamlet of Act V. And Hamlet's changing concept of death—from an escape, through a mystery and a terror, to a still-mysterious felicity and silence—becomes not a puzzle but a reflection and revelation of his changing faces as he moves from disillusionment, through confusion, to partial understanding and full acceptance of himself and his destined role. One approach to an understanding of the reality of Hamlet's character lies in the careful examination of the three faces which are reflected in the mirror of the play.

✿✿✿✿✿✿

Murder in the Cathedral: A Question of Structure

Anne LeCroy

EAST TENNESSEE STATE UNIVERSITY

❋❋ ❋❋ ❋❋ ❋❋ ❋❋ ❋❋ ❋❋ ❋❋ ❋❋ ❋❋ ❋❋ ❋❋

*R*itual—rite, the process of accomplishing public action with all things done decently and in order, following a set pattern of motions and words intended "to support a tradition and to satisfy some human need for community sharing." [1] Symbolically, whether a man cheers at a football game, marches with a banner at a convention or kneels to repeat a familiar prayer in his church, he participates in the event, hoping to gain some elevation of spirit or satisfaction of need when the timeless ritual has been completed.

By such definition, partly my own, some sorts of drama may also be accounted ritual. Certainly Greek drama was ritualistic in all its manifestations; medieval mystery and miracle plays were at least partly ritualistic, though the ritual quality was subordinated to interest in characterization. As complexities of plot increased, the importance of ritual lessened for the dramatist, after the early Tudor period, and has rarely been a noticeable part of British or American drama in the centuries since, until the present. Maxwell Anderson might, in some sense, be considered a ritualist, but the major playwright who has linked ritual again to drama, attempting to revive the liturgical structure, is T. S. Eliot, I suggest, and this most especially in *Murder in the Cathedral*.

Clear allusions to Ecclesiastes, the play on words "action,"

[1] John C. Condon, Jr., *Semantics and Communication* (New York, 1966), p. 101.

"suffering," "witness," and "martyr," familiar Eliot symbols of rats and beasts of prey and the turnings of the stair, the emphasis on dryness and sterility, the rhythms of the King James translation and the Anglo-Catholic Missal, chants, introits, and litanies mingling Christian and classical pagan traditions produce a ritual form. Ritual is an integral part of the Greek drama and of the medieval Latin church rite. What is more suitable for the classicist Anglo-Catholic Eliot as vehicle for presenting the last days and the death of Thomas Becket, Archbishop, martyr, and saint? The return and death of Thomas are single points in the wheel of a "timeless imagery and a persistent form." [2] The dramatis personae are embodiments of attitudes and ideas.

Whoever seeks to find a vivid drama of the relation between Thomas and Henry II would do well to refer to Anouilh's *Becket*. Eliot does not offer this; his play can perhaps entrance, possibly confuse, and even bore the audience expecting a familiar tragic action. To understand *Murder in the Cathedral* requires that the audience do much work, recognize Eliot's subtleties, and provide their own insight into his intention. Lack of familiarity with the Anglican liturgy, for example, can be a major handicap.

It is with this in mind that I have attempted to present my reasons for believing that the structure of the play is liturgical and that Eliot owes a heavy debt to the action of the Communion Service (or Eucharist) as it is presented in the Anglo-Catholic Missal. Let us proceed to a structural outline.

The audience, from the beginning, is a congregation, first observing and then participating in the sacramental act, just as the chorus first waits, passively, then shares in the action of the sacrifice. Not to realize this is to lose all sense of Eliot's purpose, to be misled by his language, paradoxes, symbols, and preoccupation with the collective unconscious of man's ritual action, combining both pagan and Christian elements into a rite of re-

[2] Paul Cubeta, *Modern Drama for Analysis,* 3rd ed. (New York, 1962), p. 434.

newal. These points are important as a part of the drama, but they are not the full substance of the drama, by any means. For Eliot, the substance of the drama is the memorial of Becket's supreme temptation, passion and sacrifice for the redemption of his people and the strengthening of their faith.[3]

The opening scene of the play is set on the steps of the cathedral, outside the sanctuary where the women of Canterbury chant dully of dryness, emptiness, the eternal round of the seasons, the petty crimes and domestic tasks that occupy the time. They fear disturbance:

> For us, the poor, there is no action,
> But only to wait and to witness. (p. 177) [4]

It would not be well if the Archbishop should return, after seven years' absence; they are miserably content, and they fear disturbance. The priests repeat the motif of "waiting" and add "King rules or barons rule." The messenger's speech provides some of the few references to history in the play. Thomas is coming and the people receive him, "Strewing the way with leaves and late flowers of the season" (p. 178). Thomas and the king have peace, but not the kiss of peace. For as the priest said earlier, "What peace can be found / To grow between the hammer and the anvil?" (pp. 177–178). The three priests provide three perspectives for Thomas' return: the first feels that it bodes no good; like the women, he wishes Thomas would stay away and not disturb the accustomed round. The second, contrarily, declares that the firm rock of God has returned and all will be well. The third provides balance, paraphrasing Ecclesiastes 12:3–6,

---

[3] Thomas died at the hands of four loyal barons of Henry II on December 29, 1170. The memorial collect and introit for his martyrdom was expunged from the vernacular prayer book in 1538 and has not been replaced since that time. It is, however, in the Anglican Missal, published in America, and in the traditional Roman Missal.

[4] Citations from Eliot in my text are to *The Complete Poems and Plays 1909–1950* (New York, 1952).

> Let the wheel turn.
> For who knows the end of good or evil?
> Until the grinders cease
> And the door shall be shut in the street,
> And all the daughters of music shall be brought low.
>
> (p. 179)

The chorus echoes the first priest's wail of doom:

> Do you realise what it means
> To the small folk drawn into the pattern of fate, . . .
> The strain on the brain of the small folk who stand to the
> doom of the house, the doom of their lord, the doom
> of the world? (p. 181)

The rhythm is that of a litany, with the repeated plaint "doom of the house, the doom of their lord, the doom of the world" like drum beats punctuating the prayer of the women. The mystery of the coming of Thomas—they cannot understand it or control their fear—and the priest scolds them, because of his own fear and lack of understanding.

"Peace," says Thomas to them at the moment of his entrance. Like the celebrant at the opening of the mass he first says "peace" and then speaks in paradoxes, as the celebrant speaks secretly before the altar of the sacred mysteries:

> They know and do not know, that acting is suffering
> And suffering is action. Neither does the actor suffer
> Nor the patient act. But both are fixed
> In an eternal action, an eternal patience.
> . . . .
>   The pattern is the action
> And the suffering, that the wheel may turn and still
> Be forever still. (p. 182)

The play on words "action," "actor," "suffering" and "patient" (*ago, actus, patior*) mystifies priests and women—there is not yet any communication between priest and people—the words might be those of the Latin liturgy, remote and unheard.

> Meanwhile the substance of our first act
> Will be shadows, and the strife with shadows. (p. 183)

The preparatory rite of entrance has been concluded, the celebrant is present and the substance of the first part of the mass is undertaken with the entrance of the four tempters—the shadows. Thomas expects the first three, for he has previously wrestled with each and emerged triumphant; their arguments now and his replies are merely reminiscences. Their varied words and rhythms, however, offer a slight relief from the solemn tone of the drama thus far.

In lilting, gay, shallow, riming lines the first tempter reminds him of the secular life of his youth—the hunt, the games, the sensual joys and worldly excesses. Thomas has no regret for their loss.

The second, alliterating and uttering profundities like a political candidate, speaks of temporal power and the old days of Chancellorship. Building metaphor upon metaphor he pecks at Thomas' pride, but Thomas will have none of him.

The third, countryman and Saxon, opposed to the Angevin Henry II, urges Thomas for the sake of his own countrymen, to lead a revolt, powerful under the cloak of his episcopal authority. "To make, then break" (p. 190), broods Thomas—this might once have been pleasant, as tearing down the temple was to Samson in Gaza. But Samson's way destroys others; if Thomas breaks, he breaks himself alone.

Most timely, after this initial statement of intent to seek martyrdom, is the entrance of the fourth tempter, the unexpected one. This one speaks aloud what Thomas has been meditating in his heart—at the turn of the stair—glory after death, pilgrims before a jeweled shrine, miracles, and the martyr saint, looking down from Heaven to his enemies in another place: "You have often dreamt them" (p. 193). And he quotes Thomas' word play on action and suffering and the patient, almost in a burlesque of Thomas' enigmatic advice to the women and priests.

The power of the priest, the power of the keys of the kingdom, the power to bind and loose, to advise and warn and exhort and dismiss and bless his congregation—has this power blinded

Thomas to his motive for return? Has he, God's appointed shepherd to the flock on earth, forgotten that he is a servant to his people, speaking to God not merely for his people but in communion with them? Has he turned away from them to murmur mysterious words to the altar while they merely can watch and wait without participating in his action? Thomas suddenly knows he has succumbed to pride, the last temptation.

Breaking in upon Thomas' silence, the chorus chants of emptiness, stickiness, the thick air. Man's life is empty, rejoin the Tempters, a batch of tawdry prizes from a carnival:

> This man is obstinate, blind, intent
> On self-destruction,
> Passing from deception to deception,
> From grandeur to grandeur to final illusion,
> Lost in the wonder of his own greatness,
> The enemy of society, enemy of himself.
>
> (p. 194)

Chorus, Tempters and priests chant a brief interchange of alternating sentence responses about the thousand ways of the coming of death. The women wail the loss of God, and speak of the ominous beasts of emptiness and death: "O, Thomas Archbishop, save us, save us, save yourself that we may be saved" (p. 196). No longer do they cry "O, Thomas, leave us."

Thomas' meditation is over and he sees his way clear:

> The last temptation is the greatest treason:
> To do the right deed for the wrong reason.
>
> (p. 196)

Power has been his growing sin—his soul's damnation—and as his power has increased, it has created pride in him. Though professedly serving the greater cause of God, he has in fact been serving his own hunger for power as God's minister:

> I shall no longer act or suffer, to the sword's end.
> Now my good Angel, whom God appoints
> To be my guardian, hover over the swords' points.
>
> (p. 197)

Now he awaits God's will, the actor becoming the patient witness, and the word "wait" carries altogether different significance from the word as the chorus used it in the opening chant. Thomas offers himself to do God's will when God appoints.

So the liturgy of the Word, the mass of the catechumens, is finished; this is the passive portion of the mass, when the congregation sit to receive instruction but take no personal part in the rite, btyond watching. The sermon, as in the Anglo-Catholic liturgy, is the last of the portions of instruction.

The sermon is an interlude of stillness in the turning wheel of the rite. Thomas' text is Matthew 2:14, "Glory to God in the highest and on earth, peace to men of good will." Within the cathedral, perhaps, but not beyond the pulpit at the edge of the chantry (the Church Militant for the chorus) he speaks, on December 25, of peace, not as the world gives. Martyrdom is his second topic, with St. Stephen, proto-martyr, as example:

> A Christian martyrdom is no accident. Saints are not made by accident. . . . A martyrdom is never the design of God; . . . for the true martyr is he who has become the instrument of God, who has lost his will in the will of God. (p. 199)

> Brethren: Every high priest taken from among men is ordained for men in things pertaining to God, that he may offer both gifts and sacrifices for sins: who can have compassion on the ignorant, and on them that are out of the way: for that he himself also is compassed with infirmity. And by reason hereof he ought, as for the people, so also for himself, to offer for sins. And no man taketh this honour unto himself, but he that is called of God, as was Aaron.[5]

And in the gradual, quoting from John 10: "I am the good shepherd: and know my sheep and am known of mine . . . the good shepherd giveth his life for his sheep."

The opening of the second part of the drama denotes passage of time in two ways: first by a choral chant on the passing of the seasons (an echo of the first choral chant) as the church year

---

[5] There is a reflection of the homily to St. Thomas of Canterbury in the American Missal, pp. 67–68.

reflects the movement of the seasons from Advent through Epiphany into Lent, to the climactic moments of Easter, the lesser climax of Whitsuntide and the long season of Trinity, concluding in Thanksgiving which gives way again to the penitential days of Advent. The seasons, the church year, and the symbol of the turning wheel are again recalled.

> The peace of this world is always uncertain, unless men keep
>   the peace of God.
> And war among men defiles this world, but death in the Lord
>   renews it,
> And the world must be cleaned in the winter, or we shall have
>   only
> A sour spring, a parched summer, an empty harvest. (p. 201)

Second, to indicate passing of three days, the priests appear, reminders of the first martyrs, carrying banners and chanting portions of the introits for St. Stephen, St. John the Apostle, and the Holy Innocents.[6]

The rough-spoken knights, the sordid particulars in person, break the silence with a demand for Thomas. The rapid exchange of conversation with them is in clear contrast to the meditation of the chorus and the chants of the priests. Thomas speaks boldly in answer to every accusation, defending his loyalty to the king and his first obligation to God. The chorus is reassured by his forthright speech: "O Lord Archbishop, O Thomas Archbishop, forgive us, forgive us, pray for us that we may pray for you, out of our shame" (p. 208). To this confession, subtly echoing the phrasing of the Penitential Order of the Anglican Liturgy, Thomas offers pardon, peace, and comfortable words:

> When the figure of God's purpose is made complete.
> You shall forget these things.
> · · · · · · · · · · · · · · ·
>   They will seem unreal.
> Human kind cannot bear very much reality.

[6] December 26, 27 and 28; see American Missal, pp. 59–65.

> . . . .
> Death will come only when I am worthy.
>
> . . . .
> They shall find the shepherd here; the flock shall be spared.
>
> . . . .
>   All things
> Proceed to a joyful consummation.[7] (pp. 208–209)

At the entrance to the high altar of the cathedral, the chorus (changed from passive and fearful witnesses to active participants in the martyrdom) chant a dirge that echoes the rhythms and phrases of a "Dies Irae," sung by a distant choir:

> We fear, we fear. Who shall then plead for me,
> Who intercede for me, in my most need?
>
> Dead upon the tree, my Saviour,
> Let not be in vain Thy labour;
> Help me, Lord, in my last fear.
>   (pp. 210–211)

The consecration, the reminder of Christ's passion and death and of His intercession for the sins of the world is here, below the surface of the words. "Dies Irae" is not merely a hymn of fear and the judgment, but a prayer to the Savior for his promise of salvation.[8]

Thomas will not bar the doors against the knights:

> It is out of time that my decision is taken.
>
> . . . .
> I give my life
> To the Law of God above the Law of Man.
>
> . . . .

[7] "The figure of God's purpose"—"the eternal design" from the liturgy: Come unto me, O ye that be blessed of my Father, and possess the kingdom, which is prepared for you from the beginning of the world (American Missal, p. 290); Lord, I am not worthy: that thou shouldest come unto my roof, but speak the word only and my soul shall be healed (American Missal, p. 299).

[8] The Canon of the Anglican Mass includes, at the time of the Consecration, the words of the Last Supper, prayer for the salvation of those who share in the memorial of sacrifice, and the promise of peace, resurrection and salvation at the last judgment (American Missal, pp. 296–300 passim).

67

> Now is the triumph of the Cross, now
> Open the door! (p. 212)

He approaches the altar as the knights, now somewhat drunk, enter the sanctuary, roaring a jazz tune:

> Where is Becket, the traitor to the King?
> Where is Becket, the meddling priest?
> Come down Daniel to the lions' den,
> Come down Daniel for the mark of the beast.
>
> Are you washed in the blood of the Lamb?
> Are you marked with the mark of the beast?
> Come down Daniel to the lions' den,
> Come down Daniel and join in the feast.[9]
>
> (p. 212)

Calmly, Thomas waits:

> I am a priest,
> A Christian, saved by the blood of Christ.
>
> . . . .
>
> His blood given to buy my life,
> My blood given to pay for His death,
> My death for His death. (p. 213)

So he consecrates himself to Christ's passion and to God and prays for Grace: "Now to Almighty God, to the Blessed Mary ever Virgin, to the blessed John the Baptist, the holy apostles Peter and Paul, to the blessed martyr Denys, and to all the Saints, I commend my cause and that of the Church" (p. 213).[10] Thomas raises his arms in elevation to the cross at the altar as the knights circle him and he becomes the still center of the turning wheel. And now the persistent symbol of the wheel is fulfilled and the bread is broken and the blood is shed in memorial of Christ's sacrifice. "Clear the air! clean the sky! wash the wind!" (p. 213), chants the chorus, making an act of contrition amid the

[9] O lamb of God that takest away the sins of the world, have mercy upon us . . . (American Missal, p. 298).

[10] The prayer in large part includes the names of those to whom the celebrant prays in personal confession (American Missal, p. 267) and a portion of the final prayers of the celebrant after the consecration of the bread and wine (American Missal, pp. 298–301).

rain of blood they now visualize—a baptism of blood that rein-
forces the baptism with water. "This is out of time" (p. 214),
they cry, using Thomas' words. The blood of purification
cleanses the foul world and strengthens the force of the church,
as the original crucifixion cleansed the world and established the
church. They share the paradoxical mingled joy and mourning
of martyrdom.

The knights hasten to defend their act in language that is
prosy, banal and common. Like a chorus in Aristophanic comedy they step out of their roles and speak to the congregation
their apologia for the murder: The church should serve the
interests of the state; the act was done by them with complete
disinterest—they have no money or other reward coming;
Thomas might have stirred a rebellion or betrayed the king and
the nation; Thomas died, a suicide while of unsound mind. They
conclude with the urgent request that the observers disperse
peacefully to their homes. The first priest, always the fearful and
doubting one, mourns the church bereft, but the third, who
seems to understand Thomas' action, declares that the church is
strong so long as men will die for it.

The distant chorus chants a "Te Deum," the concluding liturgical hymn of thanksgiving for Christ's sacrifice and promise of
redemption. The chorus, matching mood and metre, sings praise
to God. Purification and the end of sterility and empty rounds
of the seasons have been given them by Thomas' death and his
affirmation of God:

> Forgive us, O Lord.
> . . . .
> We acknowledge our trespass, our weakness, our fault; we
>   acknowledge
> That the sin of the world is upon our heads;
>   that the blood of the martyrs and the agony of the saints
> Is upon our heads.
> Lord, have mercy upon us.
> Christ, have mercy upon us.

69

Lord, have mercy upon us.
Blessed Thomas, pray for us. (p. 221)

So ends the litany of the saint and the liturgy of the Eucharist.
The action of the mass has been accomplished in praise and
thanksgiving, in awareness of sin and in promise of redemption
through Thomas' intercession—an action and martyrdom that
has been a memorial of the crucifixion.[11]

Thomas' death has fulfilled the purpose of the liturgy; his
meaning and his intention, so obscure at the first of the drama, is
made clear. From death comes life and the renewal of the earth
and the understanding of his sermon on mourning and joy. The
drama ends with peace—the peace that has been sought since
Thomas' entrance—a peace that is not as the world gives. The
women at the first had been anxious for the secular sort of peace
that existed while Thomas was gone and no one disturbed them.
Slowly they had come to understand the peace that follows only
a ritual action reminding them of the promise of God through
his son. Pity and terror have been replaced by a certainty that
God lives and the church is strong—Thomas has conquered by
his outward and visible enactment of the inward and spiritual
meaning of the Eucharist. It is therefore fitting that the structure
of such a drama be liturgical and Eucharistic.

[11] Grant, O Lord, that this holy Communion may cleanse us from every
guilty stain: and at the intercession of blessed Thomas thy Martyr and Bishop,
may be our healing unto life eternal (American Missal, p. 68).

✻✻✻

John Wesley Edits *Paradise Lost*

Ivar Lou Duncan

Belmont College

❧ ❧ ❧ ❧ ❧ ❧ ❧ ❧ ❧ ❧ ❧ ❧

I recall the enthusiasm with which I read a curious little volume in the British Museum entitled *An Extract from Milton's Paradise Lost, with Notes* (London: Printed in the year M, DCC, XCI [1791]). This little volume of over three hundred pages contains a prefatory note to the reader signed by John Wesley, London, January 1, 1763. I must confess my ignorance, for I had not known this book existed and might never have known except for my interest in eighteenth-century editions of *Paradise Lost*. I was somewhat surprised that such a dynamic religious leader could preach in the open air to ignorant mobs, and yet become also a shaper of men's literary taste. I pursued the subject and found that he became also "a historian, a biographer, a magazine editor, a writer of medical treatises, a producer of novels, a lexicographer, a translator of poems, a music critic, a philologist, a grammarian in half a dozen languages, a writer in natural philosophy, a poetry anthologist, a writer on logic, a political controversialist, an economist, an ecclesiastical historian, a Bible commentator, and one of the most thorough literary dictators in history."[1] How similar, I thought, was John Wesley to Alfred the Great and to Charlemagne, who labored to relieve their people of woeful ignorance by initiating a revival of literary interest and activity. And, I thought, too,

[1] Thomas Walter Herbert, *John Wesley as Editor and Author*, Princeton Studies in English, ed. G. H. Gerould (Princeton, 1940), p. 5.

73

how valuable it is to have someone unlock to the unlearned an understanding of the world of ideas imprisoned in books.

Wesley traveled 5000 miles and preached 500 sermons every year. And yet his publications number 372, including 30 books prepared in conjunction with his brother Charles. And as he began to publish only in the year 1733, when he was thirty years of age, this represents an average of more than seven volumes per year of his busy life. There are five classes of works, according to a German historian: poetical, philological, philosophical, historical, and theological. Mabel Richmond Brailsford says: "Partly by his writings and translations, and partly by editing the work of others, he made the world of Christian literature available to his converts. This he did at the lowest possible cost, and the whole scheme was carried out with more ease and less expense after he had set up printing presses of his own."[2]

His energy was consonant with that of his age. Wesley saw Lord Clive win India for England, and Wolfe win Canada. He saw Captain Cook open for England the many islands of the great Pacific. He saw George Washington take from her the thirteen colonies. Wesley was a contemporary of the Elder and the Younger Pitt, of Wilkes, of Junius. The effervescence of the South Sea Bubble was round his youth, the tumult of Lord George Gordon in his old age. Voltaire visited England in 1726–29, when Wesley was a student at Lincoln College, Oxford. Wesley saw the opening of the French Revolution.[3]

In the midst of this tumultuous and varied age Wesley was interested in education as the secret of permanent growth and progress. Like President Dwight D. Eisenhower, Wesley could have said: "I see no hope for the world except education, but I am most optimistic because I believe in education." Wesley believed that Christian people should have an interest, for instance, in the wider world of poetry. For the unlearned public

[2] *A Tale of Two Brothers—John and Charles Wesley* (London, 1954), p. 289.
[3] William Henry Fitchett, *Wesley and His Century, A Study in Spiritual Forces* (New York, 1908), p. 479.

Wesley selected that poetry "which might answer the noblest purposes" although it sometimes has been "prostituted to the vilest, even to confound the distinctions between virtue and vice, good and evil; and that to such a degree that, among the numerous poems now extant in our language, there is an exceedingly small proportion which does not more or less fall under this heavy censure." Wesley believed that many would agree with him in placing "a chaste collection of English poems among the chief desiderata of the age." [4]

And so in 1844 there had been published *A Collection of Moral and Sacred Poems. From the Celebrated English Authors*, in three duodecimo volumes. This work was the result of Wesley's selection from all the poets he knew except Spenser, whom he omitted "because scarce intelligible to the generality of modern readers." Of this volume Wesley had said: "This at least may be affirmed,—there is nothing contrary to virtue, nothing that can any way offend the chastest ear, or give pain to the tenderest heart. And perhaps whatever is really essential to the most sublime divinity, as well as the purest and most refined morality, will be found therein. Nor is it a small circumstance that the most just and important sentiments are here represented with utmost advantage, with all the ornaments both of wit and language, and in the clearest, fullest, strongest light."

Milton, Dryden, and Pope are here represented generously. Cowley, Congreve, Prior, Parnell, and Dyer are here. There are numerous selections from Latin poetry with translations. In addition, there is religious poetry by George Herbert, Roscommon, Norris, Watts, and Edward Young. The whole of *The Essay on Man is* presented, but Wesley explains carefully the inconsistencies with Scripture and Christian teaching. This anthology shows that Wesley's taste was at least catholic. Because of some trespassing upon copyright privileges *Moral and Religious Poems* did not go into a second edition, Wesley later apologizing

---

[4] *Moral and Selected Poems.* Dedication (London, 1844).

to Mr. Robert Dodsley and paying him for using Young's *Night Thoughts* without permission.[5] But the idea of *The Christian Library* came to Wesley and he pursued this idea, editing some fifty duodecimo volumes of something over three hundred pages each, between 1748 and 1755, when the last nine volumes left the press.

But Milton had always appealed to Wesley. Thomas Walter Herbert calls Milton Wesley's "most constant favorite."[6] So in 1763 it was natural that Wesley should select Milton's *Paradise Lost* for a special edition. This edition, as well as Wesley's *Journal* and letters, shows that of all the poets Wesley paid first allegiance to Milton. "He stood prominently among the authors read and reread at Oxford, and took his place with Horace, Juvenal, Homer, Shakespeare, and Spenser as one whose work was deemed worthy of careful connotation."[7] When the endless journeys of the itinerary had made it clear that if Wesley was to have a permanent private library it must exist at least in triplicate at London, Bristol, and Newcastle, Milton, along with Spenser, supplied the irreducible minimum of English poetry.[8]

With this background of preference for Milton, Wesley introduced his *Extract* with a letter to the Reader. He wrote:

> Of all the Poems, which have hitherto appeared in the World in whatever Age or Nation,—the Preference has generally been given, by impartial Judges, to Milton's *Paradise Lost*. But this inimitable Work, amidst all its beauties, is inintelligible to abundance of Readers: the immense learning which he has everywhere crowded together, making it quite obscure to persons of a common Education.
>
> This difficulty, almost insuperable as it appears, I have endeavored to remove in the following Extract: First, by omitting those lines, which I despaired of explaining to the unlearned, without using abundance of words: And, Secondly, by adding

[5] Richard Green, *Bibliography* (London, 1896), p. 7.
[6] Luke Tyerman, *The Life and Times of the Reverend John Wesley, M. A., Founder of the Methodists*, I, 490.
[7] *Journal of the Reverend John Wesley* (London, 1827), pp. 47 and 65–66.
[8] Herbert, pp. 75 ff.

short and easy Notes, such as I trust will make the main of this
excellent Poem clear and intelligible to any uneducated Person,
of a tolerably good Understanding.

To these Passages which I apprehend to be peculiarly excellent, either with regard to sentiment or expression, I have prefixed a star: And these, I believe, it would be worthwhile to read over and over, or even to commit to Memory.

London, January 1, 1763   John Wesley

Wesley deleted from the whole epic 8708 lines, or 17.5 percent of the original. Several passages in Book I received an asterisk as being peculiarly excellent. Wesley expanded Milton's Argument at the beginning. Then not mentioning the first five lines concerning Man's first disobedience, Wesley selected lines 18–26 (W. ll. 5–13):

> O Spirit, that dost prefer
> Before all Temples th' upright heart and pure,
> Instruct me, for thou know'st; Thou from the first
> Wast present, and with mighty wings outspread
> Dove-like satst brooding on the vast Abyss.
> And mad'st it pregnant: What in me is dark
> Illumine, what is low raise and support;
> That to the heighth of this great Argument
> I may assert Eternal Providence.
> And Justifie the wayes of God to man.

Passing over the question and answer concerning the cause of man's fall, Wesley selected lines 50 ff. (W. ll. 39 ff.):

> Nine times the Space that measures Day and Night
> To mortal men, he with his horried crew
> Lay vanquisht, rowling in the fiery Gulfe
> Confounded though immortal: But his doom
> Reserv'd him to more wrath; for now the thought
> Both of lost happiness and lasting pain
> Torments him.

Then Wesley selects lines 85 ff. (W. ll. 72 ff.):

> If thou (art) beest he; But O how fall'n! how chang'd
> From him, who in the happy Realms of Light

Cloth'd with transcendent brightness didst outshine
Myriads though bright: If he whom mutual league,
United thoughts and counsels, equal hope,
And hazard in the Glorious Enterprize,
Joynd with me once, now misery hath joynd
In equal ruin: into what Pit thou seest
From what highth fal'n, so much the stronger provd
He with his Thunder: and till then who know
The force of those dire Arms? Yet not for those
Nor what the Potent Victor in his rage
Can else inflict do I respect or change,
Though chang'd in outward lustre; that fixt mind
And high disdain, from sense of injur'd merit,
That with the mightiest rais'd me to contend,
And to the fierce contention brought along
Innumerable force of Spirits arm'd
That durst dislike his reign, and me preparing.

The next selection is lines 105 ff. (W. ll. 94 ff.):

What (if) though the field be lost:
All is not lost; the unconquerable will,
And study of revenge, immortal hate,
And courage never to submit or yield:
And what is else not to be overcome?

And again lines 143 ff. (W. ll. 130 ff.):

But what if he our Conquerour, (whom I now
Of force believe Almighty, since no less
Then such could hav orepow'rd such force as ours)
Have left us this our spirit and strength intire
Strongly to suffer and support our pains,
That we may so suffice his vengeful ire,
Or do him mightiest service as his thralls,
By right of Warre; Whate'er his business be
Here in the heart of Hell to work in Fire,
Or do his Errands in the gloomy Deep:
What can it then avail though yet we feel
Strength undiminisht, or eternal being
To undergo punishment?

And so on for fifteen selections from Book I. Actually an asterisk was placed at the end as well as at the beginning of each passage. If Wesley's readers had followed his directions in the prefatory letter, and thus, after reading and rereading, had attempted to memorize these passages, a real task would have been undertaken because actually one fifth of the whole was so distinguished.

Practically every page had some abridgement. In all, approximately two thousand lines were omitted. In nearly every instance passages were deleted because of the strange proper names therein contained. Wesley printed, for instance, only the first line of the following passage:

> Next *Chemos*, th' obscene dread of Moabs Sons,
> From *Arver* to *Nebo*, and the wild
> Of Southmost *Abarim*; in *Hesebon*
> And *Dononaim*, *Seons* Realm, beyond
> The flowry Dale of *Sibma* clad with Vines,
> And *Eleale* to th' *Asphaltick* Pool. (I. 406–411)

Often similes are omitted by reason either of a resounding effect or of the complexity of thought therein involved for an unlearned man. Note, for instance, Wesley's omission of the simile comparing the devils' swarming to the conclave:

> As Bees
> In springtime, when the Sun with Taurus rides,
> Poure forth thir populous youth about the Hive
> In clusters; they among fresh dews and flowers
> File to and fro, or on the smoothed Plank,
> The suburb of thir Straw-built Cittadel,
> New rib'd with Baume, expatiate and confer
> Thir State affairs. So thick, the serie crowd
> Swarmed and were straitn'd. (I. 768–776)

Sometimes Wesley converted long sentences into short ones. He could make, for example, two pentameter lines out of three of Milton. As, for instance,

> . . . our better part remains
> To work (in close design.) by (fraud or) guile
> What force effected not: that he (no less)
> At length (from us) may find, who overcomes
> By force, hath overcome but half his foe.

According to the preface nearly all of Wesley's deletions were for the purpose of making the poem more universally understandable. But Wesley also was careful to delete all passages of questionable theological or religious import. To avoid any questioning about God's allowing Satan to do what he would, Wesley omitted:

> That with reiterated crimes he might
> Heap on himself damnation, while he sought
> Evil to others, and enrag'd might see
> How all his malice serv'd but to bring forth
> Infinite goodness, grace and mercy shown,
> On Man by him seduc't, but on himself
> Treble confusion, wrath and vengeance pour'd.
>
> (I. 214–220)

Sometimes Wesley made adjustments in a pentameter line, adding or omitting to make the sense clear, but consciously keeping it a pentameter.

The Notes at the end of each book were of various kinds. Sometimes they were definitions, as, for example, the note on Wesley's verse 118, *Heavens perpetual king* in lines 128–132 of Book I:

> O Prince, O chief of many Throned Powers,
> That led th' embattld Seraphim of Warr
> Under thy conduct, and in dreadful deeds
> Fearless, endangr'd *Heav'ns Perpetual King.*

Wesley's note is: "So he terms him, not Eternal: Endeavouring to distract as much as possible from his everlasting Dominion, as if He had only reigned from Time immemorial."

Verse 144: "*Cherubim* are the second Order of Angels."

Verse 154: *His ministers of Vengeance.* "To veil his shame,

Satan ascribes his Fall to the whole Host of Angels: But Raphael, Book VI, to the Messiah alone."

Verse 349: *Thammuz came next.* "Thammuz, or Adonis, was the god of the Sidonians, slain by the wild boar in Mount Lebanon, from which the river Adonis descends. At a certain season of the year, about the Feast of Adonis, this is of a bloody colour, occasioned by a sort of Minim or red earth, which rains wash into it. The women then made loud lamentations for Adonis, supposing that it was discoloured with his blood."

Book II contains the Argument and 19 selected passages with ample transitions. The number of lines deleted is comparable to that of Book I. A note on verse 652 illustrates how Wesley injected theological implications into his explanations. *A goddess arm'd out of thine head I sprung:* "As the Heathen Poets supposed *Minerva*, the Goddess of Wisdom, to have come out of the Head of *Jupiter:* Probably from some imperfect Tradition, concerning the Son of God."

Verse 853: *Pour'd out by Millions.* "So it might seem to him, while Confusion was worse confounded. But it was the Messiah alone who did all."

Book III contains the Argument expanded and nine selected passages. The note on verse 538 *That roll'd orbicular* is: "Those Forms are supposed to be that to the Stars which our Spirit is to us. They *roll orbicular*, that is, move circularly." The note on *Triform* is: "Of three forms, increasing at full, and decreasing."

Book IV contains the Argument extended and simplified, sixteen quotable passages so marked, and seventy notes. The note on verse 867 is interesting. *His golden Scales:* "Libra or the scales, is one of the 12 signs, through which the Sun moves yearly: between Astrea (or Virgo) and the Scorpion. This also alludes to the words spoken to Balshazzar. Thou art weighed in the Balance and found wanting."

Book V contains seven starred quotations for memorization and 60 explanatory notes; Book VI contains 6 quotations designated for memorization and 55 notes; Book VII contains 6 recommended quotations and 60 notes; Book VIII (p. 201) 8 quotations and 20 notes; Book IX (p. 221) 11 quotations and 65 notes; Book X (p. 255) 8 quotations and 49 notes; Book XI (p. 287) 11 quotations and 53 notes; Book XII (p. 316) 4 quotations and 19 notes.

Paradise Lost was thus introduced to those who otherwise might not have known it. Arnold Nash describes the educational picture of the time:

> In the early decades of the century education for the poor was non-existent. For the rich it rested upon a confusion of flogging the body with training the mind. The poor in the countryside wallowed in superstitious ignorance, peopling hill and dale with goblins and fairies. In the towns the nearest approach to education, apart from what a child learned in his own home, was the apprenticeship system. The evil conditions under which children labored were not the monopoly of the Industrial Revolution. Daniel Defoe noticed that in places as far apart as Somerset, Essex, and Yorkshire, children of four or five years of age earned their own living.
>
> The education of women of the middle and upper classes was sadly lacking. The satirist Swift was not indulging in irony but reciting plain fact when he bewailed the ignorance of the daughters of gentlemen. They learned from their mothers to read and write and to sew while they waited for their fathers to obtain husbands for them by a practice of open and blatant barter.
>
> A boy, if he had energy and intelligence, was more fortunate. If he was the son of a lord he would have a resident tutor, often a Huguenot refugee. If his family were on the next lower rung of the social and economic ladder, then a neighboring parson would act as visiting tutor. Lower down the social scale still, the squire's children would attend the local grammar school and mix with boys coming from the homes of the wealthier tenant farmers, shopkeepers, and merchants. G. M. Trevelyan, the recent regius professor of modern history at Cambridge, records that not one of his predecessors from 1725 to 1773 delivered one lecture, while Trevelyan's colleague at Oxford, Sir Charles Oman, points out that at the senior university four out of

twenty professors lectured once a week and if the rest entered at all they did so only once a term.[9]

In Wesley's educational program he saw that to meet the exigencies of his time he must require of his helpers, the leaders of his educational crusade, that they be students as well as energetic workers. No man could hate ignorance more than did Wesley. To force upon his busy helpers the habits and temper of students he admonished them "to rise at four in the morning, to meditate from four to five in the morning and from five to six in the evening, to pray, and read, partly the Scriptures, with Notes on the New Testament, partly Kempis and the Instructions for Children, and partly the clearly practical parts of the Christian Library. Wesley further admonished that from six in the morning till twelve (allowing an hour for breakfast), that they read in order, with much prayer, Bishop Pearson on the Creed, Mr. Boehm's and Nelson's Sermons, the remaining parts of the Christian Library, and other tracts and poems, *Paradise Lost*, and Professor Frank's Works." [10]

In the *Discipline* of 1784–1787, we find this admonition: "Whenever there are ten children in a Society, spend at least one hour with them twice a week. And do this not in a dull, dry, formal manner, but in earnest, with your might. 'But I have no gift for this?' Gift or no gift, do it, else you are not called to be a Methodist preacher. Do it as you can, till you can do it as you would. Pray earnestly for the gift and use the means for it, particularly study the children's tracts." [11]

Wesley's literary work suffered from haste. He was a tireless and omnivorous reader and read under impossible conditions. "And betwixt duty finished and duty beckoning, he went, book in hand, and read as he went . . . . But his reading had the vice of haste. It bred swift and hurried judgments, born of half-

[9] "The England to Which John Wesley Came," *Methodism* (Nashville, 1913), pp. 13 ff.
[10] Fritchett, pp. 368–369.
[11] Arlo Ayers Brown, "Methodism's Educational Activities," *Methodism* (Nashville, 1913), p. 179.

knowledge . . . . It must be remembered that his books, when they were not controversial accidents, were written for the constituency of his own followers—a great, docile, untaught multitude, who had towards Wesley a dumb and filial reverence, and for whom Wesley had the protecting concern of a father. He would put all literature within their reach; and to do it he must translate it into their language. So he was forever condensing, abridging, and publishing books for his people. But his methods were hurried." [12]

Fritchett says that Wesley, in literature, was a fiddle with one string. "He had only one note." [13] But, as William R. Cannon observes, his mission did not often carry him "among the cultivated and the learned. Rather he was assigned by Providence to the task of preaching the Gospel of salvation to miners and day laborers, to those who manned the factories of Bristol and inhabited the dingy slums of London and other large cities of England." [14]

Wesley's problem of editing texts is noticeable today, and similar questions arise as to the solution of the problem. Do we not find translations of Chaucer adorning our college library shelves and enticing sophomores to an easier, and so, a more royal, road to learning? And we recall that John Dryden once translated Chaucer for his age. Do we not have Manly's abridged edition of Chaucer for schools, and are not all salacious passages deleted? Are there not comic books that introduce Uncle Remus in a form palatable enough to satisfy any appetite for reading Joel Chandler Harris? Do we not find comic books to tell Bible stories that otherwise would go unnoticed? But, more parallel perhaps, is the common practice among sophomore survey anthologists to delete so much that only two books of *Paradise Lost* are left by which future American citizens are led to think that Satan is the hero of our great epic because he embarks, at the

[12] Fritchett, p. 451.
[13] Fritchett, p. 483.
[14] "Accomplishments to Wesley's Death," *Methodism* (Nashville, 1913), p. 28.

end of Book II, upon a daring adventure through Chaos to find a new world. If our sophomores are inspired to go on and find an unabridged edition not only of *Paradise Lost* but also of *Paradise Regained*, the meaning of their great epic may become clear to them. But if not, what a sad failure we are in guiding college students, not the underprivileged to whom Wesley directed his edition, to become "reading Christians" and, therefore, "knowing Christians." Are our college graduates able to cope with the proper names Wesley feared the British unlearned would find unpronounceable? Should they be deleted? Will our college graduates pursue the theological implications of passages for themselves and make their own glossaries of uncommon terms?

✿✿✿

Shadow and Paradox: Imagery in *The Sound and the Fury*

George N. Dove

EAST TENNESSEE STATE UNIVERSITY

Although *The Sound and the Fury* is one of the most complex novels ever written, containing many diverse elements that appear at first to be only dimly related, there is in the book a remarkable unity in Faulkner's development of the theme of degeneration and decay. It is true that the point of view shifts from one character to another almost without fore-warning, but it is also true that this shifting viewpoint adds up, at last, an immersion in reality that is uncommon in fiction. It is true, again, that the reader is introduced to the story of the Compsons first through the consciousness of an idiot, with virtu-ally no help from the writer, but any attempt to rearrange the sections and allow someone else to introduce the story will show that the thematic unity of the novel depends upon this particular ordering. Moreover, Faulkner's remarkable chronology, in which time seems frequently to stand still, and in which the past and the present are almost indistinguishably merged, contributes indispensably to the unity of the novel. In short, *The Sound and the Fury* may be considered a masterpiece of unity-in-diversity.

One element which conduces to the unity of this work is the author's careful choice of images. Although Faulkner has been frequently accused of being carried away by his own rhetoric and of decorating his style with an inordinate profusion of metaphors, it is evident that the figures of speech in *The Sound and the Fury* have been chosen in such a way as to provide, collectively, a sort of substructure to the novel: there are images which echo and re-echo from the consciousness of one character to another in such manner as to establish spiritual and emotional kinships between the people who use them; there are "clusters" of images which center around certain ideas and involvements and thereby reinforce them; and there is a notable use of images that attain depth in character.

I am using the term "image" in the sense in which Caroline Spurgeon used it in *Shakespeare's Imagery and What It Tells Us*, that is,

> as the only available word to cover every kind of simile, as well as every kind of what is really compressed simile—metaphor . . . , connoting any and every imaginative picture or other experience, drawn in every kind of way, which may have come to the poet, not only through any of his senses, but through his mind and emotions as well, and which he uses, in the forms of simile and metaphor in the widest sense, for purposes of analogy . . . .[1]

An image, in this sense, is not necessarily a visual picture; it may represent an experience through any of the senses, or it may be without any kind of sensory reference at all. Thus, when Quentin Compson thinks of the face of the little Italian girl as "a cup of milk dashed with coffee in the sweet warm emptiness," he employs an image that is both visual and gustatory; but when he conceives of himself as a "stalemate of dust and desire," the metaphor has almost no sensory connotations. Many of the images in *The Sound and the Fury* are elaborate similes, occupying several lines of print; others are compressed into a single word, like the "*saddest* odour" of honeysuckle, or the hull of a boat "*winking* itself along."

The Sound and the Fury is divided into four sections, each representing a different fictional viewpoint and each having its own distinctive imagery.

In Part I (dated April 7, 1928) the reader is inside the consciousness of Benjy Compson, a man of thirty-three with the

[1] Cambridge, 1952, p. 5.

mind of a three-year-old child. To Benjy's confused perception, the great agony of his life is the loss of his sister Caddy, whose marriage has deprived him of the only member of the family who really loved him. Since he is physically unable to speak, Benjy's consciousness is really sub-verbal, and what sounds like metaphor in his section is not figurative at all but the result of faulty perception. This portion of the novel is full of such figurative-sounding expressions as "the steam tickled into my mouth" and "the slanting holes were full of spinning yellow," but these are literal representations of his level of perception, just as "the pig pen smelled like pigs" is literal.

Part II (June 2, 1910) is the representation of the consciousness of Quentin Compson on the last day of his life, and it closes with his departure at midnight for suicide in the river. The scene is Cambridge, where Quentin has finished his first year at Harvard, and the time is shortly after Caddy's marriage to Herbert Head. Because this section is far richer in imagery than any of the others, most of this study will be devoted to it.

The third section of the novel (April 6, 1928), in which the point of view moves to the practical-minded Jason Compson ("the first sane Compson since before Culloden"), contains almost no imagery at all; what there is consists of trite, dull figures like "her face looked like she had polished it with a gun rag" and "I was going to dash up the street and gobble two bits worth of indigestion." In view of Jason's tough-mindedness, such expressions are appropriately in contrast with the vivid flashes of the tortured Quentin.

In Part IV (April 8, 1928) the author uses a shifting point of view, which is focused chiefly upon the old Negro cook Dilsey for approximately three-fifths of the section, and then moves back to Jason Compson. The imagery is abundant and rather consciously rhetorical while the point of view is with Dilsey, but becomes sparse and flat when it switches to Jason.

Remembering what he had suffered from his imaginary incest with his sister Caddy, Quentin Compson says, "I seemed to be lying neither asleep nor awake looking down a long corridor of grey halflight where all stable things had become shadowy para-doxical all I had done shadows . . . ." The world of shadow and paradox had indeed become Quentin's real world, and many of the images he uses are figures of stable things that have become "shadowy paradoxical."

In Part II of the novel Quentin's consciousness is clouded by four obsessions: time (a constant preoccupation with watches, clocks, chimes); the odor of honeysuckle (symbolic of his incest with Caddy); water (foreshadowing his imminent suicide by drowning); and his own shadow, which he seems to identify with himself. Around these four obsessions Quentin's tortured mind builds a veritable cluster of "shadow" images, which reflect his preoccupation with time and death.

The figure of *lateness* (with the attendant imagery of night, shadows, sleep, and autumn) might be called the dominant image of the second section of *The Sound and the Fury*. This image comes so naturally to Quentin's mind that he thinks of himself as "holding all I used to be sorry about like the new moon holding water"; a leaf on the surface of the river is "waving slow as the motion of sleep"; and even the water in the basin where he washes his face has "a round blob of twilight wobbling on it." Part II is full of such images, even though June 2, 1910, is a bright spring day. In view of Quentin's determination upon suicide, it is not surprising that the lateness-image becomes associated with his obsession with time: the clocks ticking in the jewelry store are "like crickets in September grass," and there is "that quality of autumn always" in the bells striking the hour. Similarly, this image attaches itself to the smell of honeysuckle, which is "twilight-coloured," and which he remembers as "coming up out of the darkness into my room."

Closely related to this image is that of death, which obtrudes upon his thinking about all sorts of living things: the crowd of students is like "a street full of scuttering dead leaves"; women are "like drowned things floating"; cedars have "that vivid dead smell of perfume"; and even the name "Harvard" is "a fine dead sound."

The shadow-death image is fortified by the real shadow, the objective symbol of Quentin's despair and his hatred of himself. His shadow becomes as much an obsession as time, water, and the remembered odor of honeysuckle, as he walks about the streets of Cambridge or peers into the water that will soon be his grave. Standing on the bridge he sees his shadow leaning flat on the river, "so easily had I tricked it that it would not quit me." The image of the tricked shadow appears later when he is trying to help the little Italian girl find her way home, as if Quentin by escaping his shadow were escaping from himself. Even more notable is the figure of his shadow as the object of violent hatred: "trampling my shadow's bones into the concrete . . ." and "I walked upon the belly of my shadow." This image of the shadow trod upon and crushed occurs a dozen or more times in this section of the novel. In the tortured world "where all stable things had become shadowy" Quentin himself becomes a shadow to be tricked, despised, and broken.

The complement of the shadow-lateness-death image is a whole cluster of images that are basically paradoxical similes. Just as Quentin's consciousness has come to be clouded with shadows, so his world seems to have been turned inside-out: he employs images that represent a confusion of his senses, he sees inanimate things made animate by forces outside themselves, and, conversely, the people he hates become artificial, manufactured objects.

As he approaches the hour of his suicide, Quentin uses figures that attribute to himself a kind of clairvoyance or synaesthesia. "You can feel noon," he says, and "I began to feel the water before I came to the bridge." As he feels his way into his room in the dark, his senses become confused and reversed: "hands can see touching in the mind shaping unseen door," he says, and "my nose could see gasoline, the vest on the table, the door."

Such images as these are echoes of the confused figures in the first part of the novel, where Benjy says, "I could smell the bright cold," "I could hear the roof [in the rain]," and "my hands could see the slipper, and I squatted there, hearing it get dark." These echoes establish an emotional kinship between Benjy and Quentin, as if, in his misery, Quentin has come to share the confused perception of his idiot brother.

These images of synaesthesia and clairvoyance are not unique to *The Sound and the Fury:* Darl Bundren in *As I Lay Dying,* Temple Drake in *Sanctuary* and *Requiem for a Nun,* and Joe Christmas in *Light in August* are others of Faulkner's "tortured souls" who can, figuratively, feel the visible, see the audible, and hear that which others would smell or taste. It is as if the fraternity of the lost and the damned have been admitted, through their paradoxes and confusions, to special insights denied to normal men and women.

In this world of paradox, many of the images Quentin uses in reference to inanimate objects are figures of things made animate by actions outside themselves: the dry leaves on which he and the Negroes sit "whisper a little with the slow respiration of our waiting"; his feet "wake [the echoes on the stairs] like dust." Watches and clocks are almost invariably made animate; the watches in the jeweler's window have an "assertive and contradictory assurance"; his own watch is "telling its furious lie"; the chimes striking the three-quarter hour just before his death are "measured and tranquil, serenely peremptory."

It is also part of the paradox that the people Quentin hates come to be hard, manufactured, artificial things. This is especially true of the men who have taken Caddy from him: Herbert Head is "hearty, celluloid like a drummer," and Dalton Ames is a "theatrical fixture . . . papier-mache . . . asbestos . . . not quite bronze." The same kind of image is applied to the woman in the bakery shop, who is unkind to the little lost Italian girl: she is "like something on a wire, like a cash-box in a store . . . something among dusty shelves of ordered certitudes long divorced from reality, dessicating peacefully."

Here again is an emotional kinship between Quentin Compson

and another of Faulkner's "tortured" characters. Darl Bundren in *As I Lay Dying* consistently applies to his brother Jewel, whom he hates, images of things carved, hewn, and manufactured.

I have called attention earlier to the fact that Faulkner establishes a bond between Quentin and Benjy Compson by placing in Quentin's consciousness a kind of image similar to the ones used by his idiot brother. He does much the same thing in Part IV, while the point of view is with Dilsey. Mrs. Compson, looking at the Negro woman, "could not see her save as a blobby shape without depth," and this image is reminiscent of one applied by Quentin to Dalton Ames, "coming toward us tall and flat and still." The Negro preacher in Part IV "ran and poised and swooped upon the cold inflectionless wire of his voice," just as the bakery lady is seen by Quentin to be "approaching like something on a wire." In Part IV, the clock in Dilsey's kitchen is "evincing an enigmatic profundity," and this figure is a decided echo of Quentin's watches, "each with the same assertive and contradictory assurance." These echoes establish a bond between Quentin and Dilsey, the two "sympathetic" characters in the novel. There is no such bond between Quentin and his brother Jason; when the point of view switches to Jason midway in Part IV, the echoing images disappear.

When each of his figures of speech is appropriate to the context in which it is placed; when every image contributes to the total impact of the novel; when, in short, his rhetoric is under control, Faulkner is at his best. These qualities are present in *The Sound and the Fury*, and they are also to be found in his other well-written novels, like *As I Lay Dying* and *Light in August*. One might wish that he had done as well in such a novel as *Pylon*, where the images are often awkward and badly chosen, and where the irresponsible use of inappropriate metaphor becomes at times ridiculous. However badly he may have written in his worst books, though, Faulkner's reputation as a stylist can rest secure upon such a masterpiece of writing as *The Sound and the Fury*.

❉❉ ❉❉ ❉❉

Sierra Leone—the Land and the Language

John B. Ellery

WISCONSIN STATE UNIVERSITY

Sierra Leone is a small country that hangs on the lower lip of the bulging face of West Africa. It lies between 7° and 10° north of the equator, and 10° and 13° west of Greenwich. It is squeezed by Guinea in the north and east, and pushed by Liberia in the east and south. On the west its coast extends for about 280 miles along the Atlantic Ocean. Within an area of 27,925 square miles, it houses a population of about 2,000,000 Africans, 4,000 Asians, and 2,000 Europeans and Americans. The Africans represent more than a dozen different tribes, but 60% of the Sierra Leoneans are Mende or Temne tribesmen.

Terrain features vary, ranging from swampland in the west, through extensive tropical rainforests in the south, to the rugged savanna woodlands in the north. The climate is hot and humid, with an annual rainfall of about 150", and a mean temperature of about 82°. My own unofficial records show a high of 104° and a low of 82° during the years I spent at Njala, which is located near the center of the country. From November to April the country is in the path of the harmattan, sweeping down across the Sahara; from May to October it is drenched by the southwest monsoon.

Sierra Leone has been in contact with European culture since the fifteenth century, when, in 1460, a Portuguese mariner, Pedro de Cintra, arrived in which is now called Kru Bay. He named his discovery Lion Mountains, allegedly because of the thunder that roared down at him from the mountain peaks surrounding the bay. The Portuguese dominated the scene until the following century, when the British made their appearance. By 1579 even Sir Francis Drake had decided that Sierra Leone deserved the honor of his company. In 1787, just five years after the British lost the American colonies, they raised the Union Jack over Freetown, the present capital of the country. Colonialism may be blamed for many evils, but there is small doubt that in Sierra Leone civilization began with the advent of the English.

Sierra Leone became a Crown Colony in 1808; by 1827 Fourah Bay College was founded; in 1856 the country was declared a Protectorate. Finally, on 27 April, 1961, Sierra Leone became an independent nation within the Commonwealth.

As a citizen of a former British colony I know that there are some unpleasant chapters in the history of English colonization. But I also know that she has contributed something to the health, education and general welfare of the natives of the lands she colonized. Consequently, when I look at this chaotic country today I wonder how so many could take so long to learn so little. And, whatever the answer may be to that question, I wonder how a country in which the population is at least 95% illiterate, plagued by hypocrisy and stupidity, can pretend to be a nation state.

Freetown, a city of 128,000 wretched souls crammed into 4.8 square miles, is the capital and only city of any consequence in the country. It is a city of flimsy buildings, with rotting walls and rusted tin roofs, lines of slummy streets, littered with mounds of refuse and numerous barefooted men, bare-breasted women, and bare-assed kids. Untidy native shops spill their wares to the very edge of the open drainage ditches that border the streets, reeking with decomposed fruit, fish and human waste. The whole sordid mess simmers in the hot sun under a greasy film of palm oil and a thick layer of grime, seasoned with the nose-pinching stench of sweat and urine. One can escape this horror for a moment by turning toward the truly beautiful beach and breathing the clean, fresh air of the Atlantic.

This, I think, is highly indicative. Africa looks best when you have turned your back on the harsh facts of its existence.

Up-country, in the bush, there is a hint of the beauty that one might hope to find. At daybreak, when the shaggy mud huts of a village are but dimly visible in the early morning mist, smoke rising up from the outdoor cooking fires, the pungent odor of African cooking, the scene framed in stately palms, interlaced with brilliant bougainvillea, frangipani and hibiscus, one may be charmed by the aura of romance, and adventure. But, all too soon, the torrid sun reveals that the mud walls are shriveled and cracked, the thatched roofs are rotten and crawling with vermin, the people are filthy and diseased.

Among the larger communities up-country are: Bo, with a population of 20,000; Makeni, about half the size of Bo; and Kenema, a town of about 7,500. Many, but by no means all, of the towns and villages are accessible by road most of the time. A small part of the road system is poorly paved; the rest of it is unpaved, raw laterite that is ruinous to both passengers and vehicles. During the rainy season, the roads are often impassable; during the dry season they are a dusty horror. Even the limited paved sections are littered with the battered hulks of vehicles that lost the gamble against the elements and the maniacal native drivers.

There is a narrow-gauge railroad that crawls—sometimes—from Freetown to Pendembu, a distance of 277 miles almost directly across the waist of the country. Passengers provide their own food and water, and with good reason. It can take as long as 24 hours to travel 24 miles on this train which, as the natives say, "mostly don't go."

Communication is always difficult and often impossible up-country. Telephone and telegraph service is largely limited to Freetown, and even there one can expect little. Up-country stations are few in number and offer about a 50-50 chance of making contact. At Njala we maintained radio contact with Kissy, a village near Freetown, and could sometimes relay phone messages to Freetown from that point. Unfortunately, a telephone message might never be delivered; a telegram could take several days to reach Freetown; mail service is erratic and postal employees are notorious for their pilfering.

Contrary to the views expressed by those who write for *Holiday* and *The National Geographic*, native villages are grotesque rather than picturesque. A more or less typical village will be situated on the bank of a river, the source of its water supply, near a road, perhaps, surrounded by deep bush and scattered palm trees. It will consist of twenty or thirty shaggy mud huts with thatched roofs of sticks and dried grass. Some may be roofed with corrugated iron sheets. These hovels are clustered haphazardly about a fairly large cleared area that serves as the village center. Nearby one will find the court bari, in which the chief administers his peculiar brand of justice and performs other court functions. Special areas will be marked off for the Poro Bush, and the Bundu Bush, where these secret societies can hold their meetings and perform their various initiation rites. There will also be a prayer ground and at least a small mud mosque. A fairly prosperous village may even boast of a primitive blacksmith shop, for tempering and sharpening machetes, and a small trading store in one of the huts.

The village center serves as a market place, with women attending to most of the selling and bartering. Locally grown fruits and vegetables are usually available, including cassava, okra, garden eggs, kola nuts, rice, cocoyam, bananas and an assortment of citrus fruits. Groundnuts are sold raw, cooked, chopped and rolled into soggy balls. Old beer bottles, plugged with coconut fibre, are used for kerosene, palm oil and palm wine, though not necessarily all in one bottle. There will also be salt, soap, sugar, smoked fish, dried tobacco leaves and matches. Sometimes there is a modest supply of small mirrors, nails, pots and pans, pails and plastic sandals. Both the quantity and the

102

quality of the stock depends on the proximity of a motor road connecting the village with a larger trading center.

The narrow streets swarm with herniated children, scabrous dogs and half-wild chickens and ducks, all of whom scavenge among the mounds of rubbish and night-soil.

Most activity takes place outdoors, except for reproduction, rest and recuperation, though this is not to suggest that these pleasures are necessarily, or even usually, restricted to sheltered areas. The simple household furnishings, consisting of a straw bed, a few benches, and possibly a table, do not hold many additional attractions. The men lounge in their raffia hammocks, and the women cluster around the cooking fires, some fanning dull embers into small flames amid the three stones that serve as a stove and the assortment of battered and blackened pots that are their only cooking utensils. Other women and children wash the "binch," prepare the rice and grain, crush cassava leaves, or keep busy with the preparation of other items on the menu. Eventually a heavy cloud of pungent smoke settles over the entire village. This serves as a signal to those who have wandered off on the numerous bush paths circumventing the village, and they come straggling back. The men will carry the inevitable machete —they call it a "matchet"—and each woman will carry a massive head-load of faggots, food or water.

The meal, whatever the time of day or night, will probably consist of joliffe rice, or plasas, or fufu, all of which are served in a glutinous mass, loaded with hot peppers. Whatever is not eaten, and that will be precious little, is tossed aside to be scavenged by the dogs and the vultures.

Sierra Leone is a land of many questions and, so far, few answers. Most observers would agree that her only salvation lies in education. Unfortunately, such a solution involves all of the nation's most serious problems. The country does not have either the social structure or the leadership necessary for the task. Equally significant is the inability of the government to finance anything resembling an adequate educational system. It is futile to speculate on the time when sufficient money and personnel will be available unless one thinks in terms of foreign resources and expatriate staff. Without such assistance the future promises nothing but continued poverty and ignorance.

This much is certain: until the people can communicate with one another in intelligible and meaningful terms, they cannot hope to communicate with the rest of the world. The basic requirement is language facility, and this brings us to another facet of the problem.

In presenting the following commentary on the use of the English language in Sierra Leone, I have made my judgments on the basis of empirical evidence on which there is, among my expatriate colleagues at Njala University College, some measure of consensus. Whatever the limitations one may impose upon subjective analysis, and there are many that might be suggested, personal opinion should not be without some value in the academic community. There is an obvious need for sophisticated linguistic research in this area, but that is not my métier, and the infinitesimally small value to be derived from the collections of quantitative data that I have examined makes me chary of any scientific pretensions contrived to give the illusion of objectivity.

Before taking up the specific problem faced by the teacher of English in Sierra Leone, I should like to offer an assessment of the broad range of factors which influence English language usage in this country.

First, there is the residue of tribal dialects. The actual number of dialects represented probably defies an accurate count. The influx of Africans from Gambia, Guinea, Ghana, Liberia, Nigeria, and other areas, has had its effect. For all practical purposes, however, most of these can be ignored. There are thirteen dialects native to the country that may be regarded as having major importance. These are: Mende, Temne, Yalunka, Loko, Limba, Koranko, Susu, Kono, Kissi, Sherbro, Krim, Gola and Vai. There are some inter-relationships, but these do not appear to be of any significance. The dominant influence probably

104

derives from the language of the largest tribes, the Mende and the Temne.

Second, Krio is the most common vehicle of expression. Although it is not literally a universal language, it is definitely the lingua franca of Sierra Leone and, notwithstanding any official declaration that English is the official language of the country, the individual's communicativeness is based on a firm command of Krio. It might be well to observe, moreover, that Krio is much more than pidgin English. Although it may be completely unintelligible, or even appear incoherent, to someone who encounters it for the first time, it is an amazingly flexible language with many delightful nuances. It has a grammar, a rhetoric, and a character that endow it with a certain linguistic elegance that cannot be denied.

Insofar as the more readily discernible obstacles to the development of "standard" English usage are concerned, the major influence can be attributed to the vocabulary and structure of Krio. To these, one may add a closely related element, the proverb, which plays a role of unusual importance in the language.

The Krio vocabulary makes it difficult for the teacher of English to develop a truly English vocabulary building program because, in addition to providing English equivalents for Krio words, he must resolve conflicts arising from peculiar verbal relationships. Perhaps this can be best illustrated by reversing the process, as it were, and allowing the reader to compare his own vocabulary associations with those of the Sierra Leone student who is attempting to learn "standard" English. Consider the following examples:

1. Distinctively Krio words that are not susceptible to comparison with their English equivalents in terms of structure or sound:

yüba	Meaning:	vulture
bòbò	"	boy
yäwä	"	bride

pete-pete	"	completely		
pȯtō-pȯtō	"	mud		

2. *Faux amis* that may be mistaken for English words which they closely resemble, but which have a distinctive meaning:

santem	Resembles:	sometime	Means:	afternoon
binch	"	bench	"	beans
feskam	"	first come	"	bring
düyä	"	do you	"	please
jesnȯ	"	just now	"	soon

3. Words that may be recognizable because they are apparently related by derivation to words that are generally known:

sabā	Meaning:	understand
saȯr-saȯr	"	cabbage
palava	"	argument
brig	"	bridge
bubē	"	breast

4. Words that are recognizable because they closely resemble English words, but have peculiarities in pronunciation and/or form:

yī	Meaning:	eye
dō	"	door
dēa	"	dear (expensive)
ivinsef	"	even if
fambul	"	family

The degree to which an appreciation of vocabulary problems is essential to the determination of larger elements of language difficulties is perceptible in the following sentences in Krio. When words are put together in typical sequence, the combinative effect is a union of conflicting elements that must surely challenge the ingenuity of any grammarian.

aü yü dun quik sō	You have come too early.
a dā gō kut jab	I am going to do a small job.
dē bes wā gō dü . . .	The best way to do it . . .
a nō sabā am	I don't understand.
ā Bō, yü dun bȯkü	You are too fat and lazy to do anything.

106

A further complication is insinuated by the Krio predilection for proverbs, the intercalation of which plays a prominent part in almost any extended discourse. The ubiquitous epigram virtually precludes any need or desire for resourcefulness in the use of language on the part of the Krio-speaking student.

tek tem kil anch sō dat yü gō se ē gut
Take time enough to kill an ant so that you can see his gut. (i.e., Do it very meticulously.)

fo mas agidē gi lepet nȯ tȯ ē na dē tin no fȯ gō gē am fȯ drink.
To mix porridge for a leopard, that is not the thing; it is giving it to him to drink that is difficult. (i.e., What you have done is easy; you have not yet done the hard part.)

ol fiya junk nȯ at fȯ kach
Old fire junk (ashes) is not hard to get. (i.e., It is not hard to get something that nobody wants.)

befȯ ē born le ē wet
Before he is born, let him wet. (i.e., Before things look too bad, let's do something.)

Finally, one must be struck by the pathetic incongruity of an educated English-speaking native immersed in a form of English that is virtually a burlesque of any recognizable facsimile of standard English, no matter what allowances may be made for regional adaptations. Thus we find an ostentatious display of prefabricated eloquence borrowed from every imaginable source. This exaggerated eclecticism might not be quite so reprehensible were it not for the lack of sensitivity that is revealed in the process. The Sierra Leonean who falls into this category does not select eloquent words and phrases, he accumulates them and scatters them throughout his speaking and writing with an abandon that is frequently shocking and often amusing. This appetite for polysyllabic profundity is demonstrated in the following statements made by college students:

I will steer clear from any pollution by unwarranted specimens of humanity.

I do not congratulate this type of words through which you offend my physiognomy.

America with her advances in space and modern amenities is guilty of complete violation of social etiquette in her attitude toward Negroes.

He is a catalyst in the operation to bring down the banner of good behavior.

Let us lift our bottles to the brink and drink to the health of our ambassador.

I must emphasize the fact that this is not a collection of "classroom boners." Wandering words and shattered syntax are much admired and regarded as the hallmark of linguistic elegance, especially among students, politicians, and journalists. The effort to demonstrate this particular type of language facility often results in a strange potpourri of "super" English, standard English and sub-standard English liberally seasoned with Krio. Examples of this can be found in any issue of the *Daily Mail*, from which the following excerpts have been taken.

Examples of the hazards of political violence baound (sic) in other African states, and will be well advised not to borrow a leaf from these troubled spots. (From a front page *Daily Mail* editorial.)

In the face of this, fellow citizen judge ye as to who was ungreatful to who.
"E hat for make you hep man keep wakin whole net when doh clean E ask you watin make you eyes red." (From a published statement by a newspaper editor and political leader.)

Many a time people ask other people to make apologies but the Bench does not think it is in place to apologise and so it would decide in some cases to express its sympathy. (From "Kongosah Bench," a popular newspaper column.)

All the Bench could understand was that the trouble was for accommodation to sleep and somebody alleged that two of his "neighbors" had encroached on his part and I can safely say his own portion allocated to him by whom I don't know. And one of the men who really felt he was disturbed, said in his anger: "Ha nor know who rent ya to you, dis nar bus shelter, nor to you ose and you dae make noise when we wan sleep, if you continue for make noise na ya, ha go beat you." (From "Kongosah Bench.")

ARE you BERRAVED or has your wife ust (sic) given BIRTH to a child. (From *Daily Mail* Classified Advertisement Service.)

In view of these observations, it seems completely unrealistic to expect any dramatic or profound results from the present efforts to teach English in Sierra Leone. There will be progress, of course, but it will be as slow and plodding as it has been for years, unless someone can discover a conspicuously efficacious teaching method.

For my part, I subscribe to the theory that language facility must spring from practical expediency, a circumstance that is vigorously opposed by the persistence of Krio and the elusive influence of the other language elements that have been noted. A start could be made by insisting on standard English usage by students, faculty and administrators in all colleges. I should like to see the same discipline extended to all schools, as well as public offices and officials. A certain flexibility could be permitted at first, with a gradual tightening of requirements. Many will challenge the practicality of such pressure tactics, but I am convinced that the seriousness of the problem demands the use of strong measures. Because I was a professional military man long before becoming a militant professor, I have a great appreciation for the dramatic impact of a frontal attack. I sometimes feel that many of our best qualified teachers spend too much time in the center of the whirling sphere of ideas. What is needed in Sierra Leone is a supply of such teachers, provided that they are now prepared to venture to the outer edges, where the momentum is greatest and the collision of ideas most resounding.

I am not optimistic; but, hope springs eternal. I recall the day when I discussed a student's progress in English with a Dean, who listened to me, then interrogated him in Krio; the Dean then solicited information from the Office of the Registrar via a telephone conversation in Krio; he reported the results of this conversation to me, in English. What could I say, except: dis wan ful me mot; or, as we say in standard English, How does that grab you?

❊ ❊ ❊

Kierkegaard and the Modern American Novel

Lewis A. Lawson

The University of Maryland

It was more than forty years after the death of Sören Kierkegaard in 1855 that David F. Swenson, the first American to publicize Kierkegaard's thoughts, came across a copy in Danish of the *Concluding Unscientific Postscript*, in a local library in Minneapolis. After browsing for a few minutes in the book—which contained a language familiar enough, if the ideas were totally new—Swenson took the book home, to read and reread its passages throughout the night. The first night's sitting convinced him that he should learn as much as he possibly could about the thought of Kierkegaard so that he could introduce it to his students in philosophy at the University of Minnesota.

Since there were no English texts, Swenson had first to locate and then to master Kierkegaard's many works, which were written behind so many different guises and in so many different styles. Finally, in 1914, he was ready to speak of Kierkegaard to others, in a course at the University entitled "Great Thinkers of the Nineteenth Century," the first public address in English about Kierkegaard ever given in this country, so his widow states in *Kierkegaardian Philosophy in the Faith of a Scholar*. And after he began to make lectures, Swenson began also to write introductory articles about Kierkegaard in journals that specialized either in Scandinavian or in philosophical concerns, such as *Scandinavian Notes and Studies* and *Ethics*.

Despite the sincerity of Swenson's admiration for Kierke-

gaard, it is doubtful that he alone would ever have been successful in bringing him before a large American audience. Swenson
was a scholar; thus he may have been either too retiring a
personality or too scrupulous a translator. At any rate he did not
offer any of his translations for publication, so that the only
work of Kierkegaard in English before the middle Thirties was
Selections from the Writings of Kierkegaard, edited and translated by Lee M. Hollander for the University of Texas *Bulletin*
in 1923. This work was certainly of very limited circulation.

Thus it remained for Walter Lowrie, a clergyman past the
age of retirement, to provide Kierkegaard's introduction to a
general American audience. After graduating from Princeton
University and being ordained as a minister in the Episcopal
Church, Lowrie served from 1907 to 1930 as rector of St. Paul's
American Church in Rome. About 1927 he began to read the
work of Karl Barth in German. Since Barth relied rather heavily
on Kierkegaard, Lowrie soon began to read him in a German
translation. And when Lowrie returned to Princeton in 1930, he
retained his interest in Kierkegaard, so much so that at the age of
sixty-five he taught himself Danish in order to grasp Kierkegaard's thought as completely as possible. As he became more
familiar with the work, he became more vocal about its value for
his contemporaries; he proclaimed in 1932 in *The Theology of
Crisis:* "For what reason have we so many universities? Is it to
ensure that studious youth shall be shielded from contact with
contemporary thought?"

In December of 1934, an Englishman, Alexander Dru, wrote
to Lowrie to suggest that the two of them be responsible for the
translation of Kierkegaard into English. Receiving Lowrie's as-
sent and encouragement, Dru approached the Oxford University Press, to propose to Charles Williams, the editor whose own
literary significance was just receiving wide acknowledgment,
that his firm assume the responsibility of publishing the English
translation of Kierkegaard. Williams sent Ralph Binfield to the
British Museum to discover what there was of Kierkegaard's in

English. Then he began to read what little he could find about this man whose ideas seemed all of a sudden so pertinent.

By December of 1935 Williams was ready to recommend to Sir Humphrey Milford, the publisher, that the Press undertake the responsibility. His recommendation was accepted, and an "incredible accomplishment," as Lowrie termed it in his Introduction to his translation of Kierkegaard's *Christian Discourses*, was begun, an accomplishment only achieved through the "wisdom and audacity" of the Press and more particularly of Charles Williams. But so taken with Kierkegaard was Williams that he not only supervised the publication; he was also soon lecturing on him at the City Literary Institute, the first public lectures on him in England, declares Alice Mary Hadfield in *An Introduction to Charles Williams*.

Sometime earlier Lowrie and Swenson had also begun a fruitful correspondence. At Lowrie's urging Swenson had decided to undertake the translation of one of the works; he chose *Philosophical Fragments*, rather than one of the better-known works, because his primary interest in Kierkegaard lay in the man as philosopher, not as theologian. Princeton University Press published the translation in May of 1936; Oxford University Press followed with its publication in December of the same year. With this publication there began a magnificent decade of translation.

There was a general agreement among Lowrie, Swenson, and Dru about each man's responsibility. After *Philosophical Fragments*, Swenson was to undertake the *Concluding Unscientific Postscript* and then *Either/Or*. After his translation of Haecker's biography and the translation of *The Journals of Kierkegaard* (1938), Dru was to translate *The Concept of Dread*. And after the publication of his biography *Kierkegaard* in 1938 (which he dedicated to Swenson and which, he acknowledged in the Preface, owed much of its stylistic quality to Williams), Lowrie was to undertake *The Sickness Unto Death*.

But Dru's participation in the war and Swenson's debility left

much the largest burden for translating Kierkegaard upon Lowrie, now seventy years old. In the early Forties he translated
Christian Discourses (1939), *The Point of View for My Work
as Author* (1939), *Stages on Life's Way* (1940), *The Sickness
Unto Death* (1941), *Fear and Trembling* (1941), and *Repetition* (1941), just to mention the best known of his fifteen or so
translations of Kierkegaard. And since Dru had not finished his
translation of *The Concept of Dread* before he was wounded in
the earliest days of the war and retained on active duty after his
recovery, he had to relinquish the task to Lowrie, who was able
to finish it by 1944. Then, too, Lowrie had to assume the task of
the *Concluding Unscientific Postscript* (1941) after Swenson's
death in 1940. Moreover, he translated all of Volume II, *Or*, of
Either/Or (1944), Volume I, *Either*, being completed by Swenson's widow.

It is at this point that W. H. Auden stepped forward to
become Kierkegaard's advocate in America. In the May 15,
1944, issue of *The New Republic*, Auden offered a review of
Either/Or entitled "A Preface to Kierkegaard." This review did
not, however, represent Auden's first meeting with Kierkegaard.
Back in 1938 Auden had visited the offices of the Oxford University Press, probably, as Monroe K. Spears suggests in *The
Poetry of W. H. Auden*, to discuss the editing of the *Oxford
Book of Light Verse*. There he met Charles Williams and suffered a kind of charismatic experience: as Auden himself describes the event in *Modern Canterbury Pilgrims*, "Shortly aft-
erwards, in a publisher's office, I met an Anglican layman, and
for the first time in my life felt myself in the presence of
personal sanctity." From his experience came his religious decision: "So, presently, I started to read some theological works,
Kierkegaard in particular, and began going, in a tentative and
experimental sort of way, to church."

There was little else of Kierkegaard but Dru's selections from
The Journals for Auden to read. Those he read closely, however, so closely that the notes he provided for his next long

116

poem, *The Double Man* (1941), several times quote directly from Dru's translation. Nor is this the extent of the use of Kierkegaard in the poem. Both Edward Callan ("Auden's *New Year Letter:* A New Style of Architecture," *Renascence: A Critical Journal of Letters,* XVI [1963], 13–19) and Justin Replogle ("Auden's Religious Leap," *Wisconsin Studies in Contemporary Literature,* VII [1966], 47–75) see the influence of Kierkegaard in the ideas, the imagery, and even the structural devices of this poem and of Auden's subsequent long poems, *For the Time Being* (1944) and *The Age of Anxiety* (1947).

All during the Forties Auden apparently retained a deep interest in Kierkegaard. For, in addition to his reliance upon Kierkegaard's works for the creation of his poetry, Auden seems to have been synthesizing for presentation the basic ideas that recur throughout the Kierkegaard canon. These Auden collected in *The Living Thoughts of Kierkegaard,* published in 1952. Drawing upon the best known of Kierkegaard's works, that is, primarily the "aesthetic" as opposed to the "edifying," the "indirect" as opposed to the "direct" communications, to use Kierkegaard's own distinctions, Auden offered excerpts under several rubrics: Prefatory Aphorisms; The Present Age; The Aesthetic, the Ethical, and the Religious; The Subjective Thinker; Sin and Dread; Christ the Offence; Epilogue. And in his Preface Auden offered a clarification of Kierkegaard's relationship to what commonly passes as the existential attitude and of his significance both to his own time and to ours.

Auden's collection of excerpts may be said to be symptomatic of, not necessarily solely responsible for, a rapidly developing general awareness of Kierkegaard in America in the early Fifties. It is true that theological and philosophical journals contained some mention of him just before World War II, a mention fostered by students returning from Europe and by refugee scholars from Germany. But not until the publication of most of his works between 1939 and 1944 and not until the publicity of French existentialism in this country just after the war, with the subsequent discussion of its reliance upon the thought of Kierkegaard, did a rather general knowledge of his work begin to permeate the American literary establishment.

When his ideas were given frequent attention, though, with their vivid catchwords such as "the leap of faith" or "the sickness unto death," a good many writers began to realize the technical, as distinguished from the religious/philosophical, contribution that his material could make to their craft. The two main contributions would be, I think, a new method for the analysis and development of character and a new structure for the achievement of narrative progression.

The novelist has always been interested in techniques of establishing motivation, of exploring the psychology of his characters. Both Marx and Freud provide concepts that novelists can utilize in the depiction of character; hence modern literature contains novels about the economic man and the psychological man. What Kierkegaard offers, especially in such works as *The Concept of Dread* and *The Sickness Unto Death*, is an exploration of the dreading and despairing man, the agonizing man. And since dread and despair are almost universal and much more easily observable to any layman than is a sense of one's purported victimization by economically or psychologically determining forces, Kierkegaard will likely prove to be more useful to the novelist in the long run than will be Marx or Freud. Kierkegaard offers to the novelist, in other words, a more "human," yet no less complex, exploration of human sensibility, than does either Marx or Freud.

The novelist has always been interested, too, in techniques of achieving the representation of linear movement. Early novelists may have taken it for granted that action in novels, supposedly like life itself, naturally progressed. Life moves forward in time, it would appear, and the early novelists quite without thinking about it almost always utilized a simple straightforward chronological progression. But modern novelists, more and more aware of the ambiguities of the concept of time, of the false distinctions between past, present, and future, have been deeply attentive to other methods of representing levels of temporal reality in fiction. In *Ulysses*, for example, Joyce maintains an almost slavish attention to chronological time, while at the same time employing the historical cycle proposed by Vico and the Homeric parody which he had devised for himself. In *The Sound and the Fury* Faulkner, while confusing chronological representation of time, utilizes, at least according to some readers of the novel, the scheme of the partitioning of the psyche devised by Freud.

Kierkegaard, as well, offers many schemes of progression that are attractive to the novelist. The reason for these many schemes lies in Kierkegaard's basic view of man: man is a creature who is always in a state of becoming. Human existence is not static, incorporate within itself. One does not stand still; one continues to face forward into a new condition, his crucial decision always to be made, never having been made. Kierkegaard's most encompassing scheme of progression is that of the spheres of existence, a scheme which is best illustrated in *Concluding Unscientific Postscript*. Man lives in either the aesthetic or the ethical or the religious sphere. Most men remain in the aesthetic sphere all their lives, caught up in the pursuit of sensual satisfactions, with only a vague hint of and longing for the higher spheres. Some men struggle upward to achieve the ethical; a few even achieve the religious. Each sphere has of course its own special characteristics; each of the two junctures between spheres likewise has its own peculiarities. So detailed and rich in suggestiveness are these various stages or states of existence that the full scheme would support the construction of a novel or even a series of novels, indeed.

Then, too, the various psychological states analyzed by Kierkegaard are volatile qualities. That is to say, in Kierkegaard's religious psychology one is never in an absolute, unvarying, eternally fixed state, either of damnation or of grace. This view is best seen in *The Sickness Unto Death* and *The Concept of Dread*. One is never, for example, in a state of absolute, irredeemable despair. One lapses into despair that is unaware of itself; one becomes aware, then attempts to defy despair; one willingly despairs; one gains the faith that is the only antidote to despair. The stage at which one stops his journey is entirely an individual matter—but the road is the same for all. This scheme is laid out in minute detail in *The Sickness Unto Death*. And a similar analysis is given of dread, though not quite so detailed, in *The Concept of Dread*.

The year of Auden's *Living Thoughts of Kierkegaard*, 1952, also noted the direct use of Kierkegaard's ideas in the American novel. Interestingly, both novels of that year containing references or allusions to Kierkegaard are by Negroes, Ralph Ellison and his older sponsor, Richard Wright. Ellison simply utilizes Kierkegaard to deepen his own meanings while Wright seems to relinquish the priority of his own experience to the preconceived structure derived from Kierkegaard. The immense success of Ellison's *Invisible Man* and the almost total failure of Wright's *The Outsider* certainly result in part from the method which each author employs in addressing himself to the consciously appropriated material from Kierkegaard.

Using *another* strategy of narrative progression (which is based, as he acknowledges in *Shadow and Act*, upon Kenneth Burke's concept of the movement from purpose to passion to perception), Ralph Ellison consequently enlists only limited, though significant, aid of Kierkegaard. Early in *Invisible Man*, in the Prologue, the nameless protagonist accounts for his hibernation, his retreat from society, and then asks himself a rhetorical question about his desire to write of the events that led to his retreat: "Could this compulsion to put invisibility down in black and white be thus an urge to make music of invisibility? But I am an orator, a rabble rouser—Am? I *was*, and perhaps shall be again. Who knows. All sickness is not unto death, neither is invisibility." The "sickness unto death" is, of course, Kierkegaard's description of despair. Ellison is thus suggesting, from the very beginning, that the quest of his protagonist will be successful; and so it is, after he is able to arrive at a dramatic, oppositely oriented redefinition of the nature of his quest. In the Epilogue the protagonist summarizes his failure in attaining the goal of his original quest: "The fact is that you carry part of your sickness within you, at least I do as an invisible man. I carried my sickness and though for a long time I tried to place it in the outside world, the attempt to write it down shows me that at least half of it lay within me." Recognizing that self-definition is not accomplished by the conferral of identification by external agencies, the protagonist thus realizes that his despair does not result from his failure to be accepted by society. On the contrary, whatever despair he feels results from *his* failure to accept and have faith in himself. For Kierkegaard, the only antidote to despair is faith. Accepting this uncompromising argument, the protagonist determines to show his faith in himself by returning once more to the world which has spurned him. As he says, "Live you must, and you can either make passive love to your sickness or burn it out and go on to the next conflicting phase." Constructing his options in the Kierkegaardian *either/or*, he intends to burn out his sickness by the process of writing of it and to look forward to the next sphere or phase of existing in an ever-changing, ever-challenging universe.

In *The Outsider* Richard Wright utilizes materials which he derived from Sartre and Camus (though inadequately, chiefly because he is content to allow his characters to proclaim, rather than think or act out their philosophies). Even more, as Kingsley Widmer points out ("The Existential Darkness: Richard Wright's *The Outsider*," *Wisconsin Studies in Contemporary Literature*, I [Fall 1960], 13–21), does Wright rely on Kierkegaard, for the novel is heavily dependent upon a structure provided by the categories of dread described in *The Concept of Dread*.

Furthermore, the central irony of the novel is based upon an observation made rather early in *The Concept:* "He who through dread becomes guilty is innocent, for it was not he himself, but dread, an alien power, which laid hold of him, a power he did not love but dreaded—and yet he is guilty, for he sank in the dread which he loved even while he feared it." Cross Damon, the protagonist, is precisely caught in Kierkegaard's paradox. He had been born into the Christian tradition; his mother had named him Cross after "the Cross of Jesus." Yet Cross refuses to accept the gift of Christianity, seeing it more as a burden, since it involves the acceptance of Original Sin and the consequent universal guilt and sense of dread. Rather he seems to think of himself as Adam the innocent, Adam before the Fall. Hence he stubbornly maintains his innocence throughout his life, even as the dread he cannot dispel forces him into ever more violent acts.

Cross makes symbolic gestures toward losing his dread-dominated self by assuming a series of aliases. But he cannot thus escape himself and he eventually becomes, as his last name would indicate, a demon. The demonic is a state described in both *The Concept of Dread* and *The Sickness Unto Death* as being farthest from God. And this is the point that Cross reaches, for he becomes, so his captor Ely Houston tells him, his own god. Thus he begins to judge others and execute them, with no thought as to his right before God to commit such acts. When, in time, he is fatally wounded in retribution, he is still unwilling to acknowledge his guilt before God, and he is therefore still in a state of dread (which poses as innocence), as he maintains to the end: "In my heart . . . I'm . . . I felt . . . I'm *innocent* . . . ."

Since 1952 there has been a fairly steady use of Kierkegaard in American fiction. As it would be expected, some of the usage has been rather incidental. J. D. Salinger, for example, allows Buddy Glass to quote *The Sickness Unto Death* as a motto for *Seymour, An Introduction* (1959): "It is (to describe it figuratively) as if an author were to make a slip of the pen, and as if this clerical error became conscious of being such. Perhaps this was no error but in a far higher sense was an essential part of the whole exposition. It is, then, as if this clerical error were to revolt against the author, out of hatred for him, were to forbid him to correct it, and were to say, 'No, I will not be erased, I will stand as a witness against thee, that thou art a very poor writer.' " But the choice of this motto seems dictated only by Buddy's recognition of the difficulty of presenting an adequate description of anyone in art. Salinger, in other words, does not seem to be employing the quotation for any religious or philosophical significance. A far more meaningful use is John Updike's adoption of Kierkegaard's *angst,* mentioned in *The Concept of Dread,* for the name of his main character in *Rabbit, Run* (1961). For Harry "Rabbit" Angstrom is precisely that kind of man who is impelled forward by dread.

Carson McCullers was also drawn to *The Sickness Unto Death* in *Clock Without Hands* (1961). Her theme here is still the one to which she was always attracted, the isolation of the human heart, for she emphasizes that J. T. Malone, one of the chief characters (who is appropriately named), is suffering not only from a deadly disease but also from a deadly disease called life. Malone is said to have picked out the Kierkegaardian study from a hospital library cart, and certain passages from it occupy his consciousness from time to time thereafter. But still the use of Kierkegaard seems extraneous and intrusive, for Malone does not need Kierkegaard's unique point of view to persuade him of the rightness of his final action, and thus the inclusion of the Kierkegaardian material simply weakens an already unsatisfactory novel.

One of the most skillful uses of Kierkegaard has been William Styron's reliance upon the scheme of the stages of despair found in *The Sickness Unto Death* in his novel *Set This House on Fire* (1960). The clue is in the protagonist's name, Cass Kinsolving, who is discovered in a miserable state because he cannot establish the relationship between himself and his self, between that which is personal and that which is impersonal. In this state Kinsolving depends upon drink and drugs to keep himself from approaching any degree of self-awareness. Then one day it happens that he is overcome for a moment by a vision of eternity, so that he passes from the condition of immediacy, of unconscious despair, to the condition of conscious despair, which is, Christianly speaking, infinitely better. With that awareness preying upon him, Kinsolving desperately begins to employ the various evasions described by Kierkegaard that purport escape from consciousness. One method is to commit suicide, in the hope that destruction of body implies destruction of spirit. Kinsolving dreams of the act, but dreams also of being imprisoned for an infinite term. Thus he concludes that in committing suicide he might only be guaranteeing himself to eternal despair. It seems to follow, then, that if it is the eternal which is at the root of one's problem, that troublesome quality should be denied; so Kinsolving persists in his drunkenness and his running until one morning he awakens to scream *"Non c'è Dio!"* But such a device offers no permanent or authentic relief, for only faith can provide an antidote to Kinsolving's sickness. Thus it is that he must continue to suffer until he has admitted the sources of his sense of guilt that lie far back in his Southern past. Only then does he begin to feel the stirrings of faith and hope.

The writer who has most recently used the strategies of Kierkegaard is Walker Percy, author of *The Moviegoer* (1961) and *The Last Gentleman* (1966). Indeed, so impressed by Kierkegaard has he been that he has apparently decided to conduct his career according to a Kierkegaardian evasion. In *The Point of View for My Work as Author*, Kierkegaard admits that much of his work was couched in the "indirect approach," that he had hoped to catch his readers aesthetically and then, before they realized it, say something significant to them about their human existence. Because of an allusion near the end of *The Moviegoer*, there is good reason to suspect that Percy abandoned non-fiction after some years of practice and began to write novels in the hope of employing them "aesthetically."

The protagonist of *The Moviegoer*, Binx Bolling, is an inhabitant of Kierkegaard's "aesthetic mode," as Percy has admitted

(Ashley Brown, "An Interview with Walker Percy," *Shenandoah*, XVIII [Spring 1967]). Thus he is much like the "aesthetic man" described in *Either/Or* as he tries to gain genuine satisfaction in a world that is limited only to physical pleasure. But, also in the spirit of Kierkegaard's conception of man as a quester, Binx goes forward, meeting each day's demands as best he can, alert to any hint that there might be more to it than what he calls "the Little Way." His very persistence seems to reward him at the conclusion when he manages through sheer doggedness to ascend to the next plateau, that of the "ethical mode," where he demonstrates enough selflessness to take care of another desperate soul.

Similarly, Will Barrett, the protagonist of *The Last Gentleman*, appears to make his way from the "ethical mode" to the "religious mode." Although cast in a highly humorous garb (and here Percy is at his most aesthetically captivating), the ascent is not made without peril and confusion. Nor is the conclusion free of ambiguity. But just as Binx's name indicates the unknown quantity that he has been to himself all of his life ("been X"), so Will's name becomes at the end an indicator of his changing state. For at the conclusion he determines to bear all things, believe all things, in order to achieve Kierkegaard's Religion B, the religion of transcendence. Thus virtually his last words are "I, Will Barrett . . . ."

It is, of course, impossible to predict just how much longer American novelists will feel drawn to the writings of Sören Kierkegaard. The impact of novelty should certainly be lessening, so that it might be thought that such use, if it results only from a fad, will soon disappear. On the other hand, if American novelists continue to set as their task the exploration of the deprived and stunted spiritual state of their countrymen, then the arguments and strategies of Kierkegaard will still be heard in the American novel.

❊❊❊

Emily Dickinson's "Test of Trouble"

Robert J. Higgs

EAST TENNESSEE STATE UNIVERSITY

The basic idea of psychological time is as old as "myths, legends, and fairy tales in which there are more times than one, a relativity of times."[1] Probably since he invented instruments for measuring time, man has been conscious of the fact that objective time quite often seems at variance with the passing of time actually experienced. It was not until the 1890's, however, that psychological time came into being as a concept to be studied and pondered by psychologists and philosophers. Generally stated, the theory holds that time is not a phenomenon of prior condition but a consequence of experience, imagination, will, and memory.[2] In other words, psychological time is graduated not by clocks and calendars but by emotion. Today we encounter the idea at every turn, in commercials, poetry, and novels. Admen ask us if we have suffered long, sleepless nights, Wallace Stevens wants to know "on what does the present rest," and in *Catch 22* one character wishes to be bored because it gives him the sense of the slow passing of time, thus making him think that he is living longer. Indeed psychological time is experiencing its finest hour.

In Emily Dickinson's day, however, the concept had not even been formulated by specialists, and her contemporaries, we believe, unlike ourselves, were not generally given to contemplation of space and time. Hence they were not as plagued with the problem of identity. Emerson, of course, thought about every-

---

[1] J. B. Priestly, *Man and Time* (London, 1964), p. 70. Subsequent references are to this edition.
[2] G. J. Whitrow, *The Natural Philosophy of Time* (London, 1963), p. 50.

thing, but he and Thoreau knew who they were.[3] Neither they nor Emily Dickinson, who for her day was so precociously involved with psychological time, would have asked such a question as that posed by the contemporary poet Alfonso Cortes:

> —Time, you and I
> Where are we,
> I who live in you
> And you who do not exist? [4]

Emily Dickinson knew who she was and where she was, but her preoccupation with psychological time foreshadowed the angst which results when poets and novelists turn to the subject today. Her "inner clock" was particularly sensitive and was never synchronized with the motions in the world. Time for her was thrown completely awry by certain ordinary events:

> I think the longest Hour of all
> Is when the Cars have come—
> And we are waiting for the Coach—
> It seems as though the Time
>
> Indignant—that the Joy was come—
> Did block the Gilded Hands—
> And would not let the Seconds by. (J635) [5]

On occasion time appeared to her as especially tractable:

> If you were coming in the Fall,
> I'd brush the Summer by
> With half a smile, and half a spurn,
> As Housewives do, a Fly.
>
> If I could see you in a year,
> I'd wind the months in balls—
> And put them each in separate Drawers. (J511)

[3] Durant H. Da Ponte, "James Agee: The Quest for Identity," *Tennessee Studies in Literature*, VIII (1963), 25.

[4] "Two Poems by Alfonso Cortes," trans. Thomas Merton, *Sewanee Review*, LXXI (Summer, 1963), 467.

[5] *The Poems of Emily Dickinson*, ed. Thomas H. Johnson, 3 vols. (Cambridge, Mass., 1963). Subsequent references are to this edition.

Quite obviously, then, time for Emily Dickinson was a state of awareness which was controlled by joy, pain, and expectation.

Psychological time can be divided into what J. B. Priestly calls Great Time and passing time. Great Time was that of "the myths, the gods, the mighty spirits" and primitive man, who "was sustained not by the meaningless passage from dawn to noon and noon to sunset, but by this Great Time, in which all creation, power, magic, existed" (p. 140). "Great Time is *all-at-once* [with] past and present and future merging and becoming one—the eternal instant." Passing time, on the other hand, is "*one-thing-after-another.*" It is, as Priestly sees it, a major cause for despair in the modern world. Modern man "feels his life is being ticked away . . . and cannot enter into any 'eternal dream time,' knows nothing of the invisible things of past, present and future, and has no such hidden source of courage and strength: He feels himself fastened to a hawser that is pulling him inexorably toward the silence and darkness of the grave" (p. 140). It is a telling comment on the contradictory nature of Emily Dickinson that both of these types of time appear in her poetry. With Andrew Marvell she always hears time's chariot hurrying near, but with William Blake she can hold infinity in the palm of her hand and eternity in an hour. But passing time in Emily Dickinson is much more evident than Great Time. Unlike Walt Whitman who lived only in Great Time, she could not ultimately free herself from passing time. "If man," says Charles R. Anderson using Alfred North Whitehead for authority, "is to break out of the bondage of time into eternity [from passing time to Great Time] it will be through the imagination of the artist rather than through the philosophical thought or religious faith."[6] Here it must be said that if there is to be an art which will ultimately free us from passing time, it must be art in the tradition of Whitman and not Emily Dickinson, for her poetry, like that of Wallace Stevens and W. H. Auden, induces a feeling of helplessness about time rather than exultation in being alive

[6] "The Trap of Time in Emily Dickinson," *ELH*, XXVI (1959), 423–424.

in it. In fact the tremendous difference between passing time and Great Time could not be better illustrated than by quoting explicit references to time by Dickinson and Whitman. "Down Time's quaint stream," says Emily Dickinson,

> Without an oar
> We are enforced to sail
> Our Port a secret
> Our Perchance a Gale
> What Skipper would
> Incur the Risk
> What Buccaneer would ride
> Without a surety from the Wind
> Or schedule of the Tide.
>
> (J1656)

We should note not only the passiveness of the verse but also a certain fear, especially when contrasted with Thoreau's happy indifference to time, a stream to "go a-fishing in," and with Whitman's aggressiveness and complete mastery of it.

> Not Time affects me—I am Time, old, modern as any,
> Unpersuadable, relentless, executing righteous judgments,
> As the Earth, the Father, the brown old Kronos, with laws,
> Aged beyond computation, yet ever new, ever with those
> mighty laws rolling . . . .[7]

Whitman, to be sure, was not oblivious to the passing nature of time. "The past and present wilt—I have fill'd them, emptied them, / And proceed to fill my next fold of the future" (p. 88). But this passing is not a draining away. It is more of a change. Time for him does not leak or gurgle on. He stands in an eternal instant, joyously filled with the past and devouring the future; and ever is he the master. "I know I have the best of time and space, and was never measured and never will be measured" (p. 46). For Emily Dickinson, however, "Time is a Test of Trouble" (J686).

---

[7] *Leaves of Grass* (Comprehensive Reader's Edition), eds. Harold W. Blodgett and Sculley Bradley (New York, 1965), p. 443. Subsequent references are to this edition.

The different attitudes toward time in Dickinson and Whitman help to explain their concepts of immortality. For Emily Dickinson immortality—and she is anything but sure of immortality—is some unfathomable, timeless state which dips ahead of her after the "Term between." For Whitman, immortality is here and now, the most certain fact about life. "I swear," he says in "To Think of Time," "that there is nothing but immortality!"

Emily Dickinson's thralldom by time can best be seen in her attitude toward the three parts of the "Term between," a lost past, an evanescent moment, and an unknowable future. Rarely do these three merge into one as they must in Great Time, and as they do in Whitman:

> I am an acme of things accomplish'd, and I am encloser
> of things to be.
> My feet strike an apex of the apices of the stairs,
> On every step bunches of ages, and larger bunches between
> the steps,
> All below duly travel'd, and still I mount and mount.
>
> (pp. 80–81)

For Emily Dickinson the past, present, and future are almost separate entities connected by the conventional flow of passing time. "Yesterday a Vagrant— / Today in Memory lain" (J1209), she says, and

> Yesterday is History,
> 'Tis so far away—
> Yesterday is Poetry—
> 'Tis Philosophy—
> Yesterday is mystery—
> Where it is Today. (J1292)

In Whitman there is a sense of immediacy about the past, but with Emily Dickinson it is mysterious, remote, a subject for philosophy, a cause for a cry of *ubi sunt*:

> Ah, said July—
> Where is the Seed—

Where is the Bud—
Where is the May. (J386)

Like Whitman, Emily Dickinson, in the strictest sense of the word, had nothing to do with lamentation, but her poetry is filled with the sadness of loss. Thus whereas Whitman gladly embraces the past as part of the present, Emily Dickinson would like to sever it completely:

How to forget!
Ah, to attain it—
I would give *you*—
All other Lore. (J433)

Indeed she makes of memory, that great reservoir of psychological time, a monster, a type of hydra:

Nor can you cut Remembrance down
When it shall once have grown—
It's Iron Buds will sprout anew
However overthrown. (J1508)

If the past is loss, the future, also separate and distinct, is all too likely to contain that which will only add to that loss; consequently, Emily Dickinson wished that there were some way to avoid it.

Oh Future! thou secreted peace
Or subterranean wo—
Is there no wandering route of grace
That leads away from thee—
No circuit sage of all the course
Descried by cunning Men
To balk thee of thy sacred Prey—
Advancing to thy Den. (J1631)

Since the poet wished to steer clear of the future, we can assume that she regarded it not as "secreted peace" but as "subterranean wo," which, after passing through the present, is added to the eighteen-thousand-year-old woe of the past.

In her very attempt to reason her way out of passing time,

Emily Dickinson only reveals her bondage to it. "Forever—is composed of Nows—" she pronounces, but in using the plural of now she shows clearly that she conceived of life not as one Great Now as Whitman did but as a series of little nows, instantaneously following one another and changing the future into the past. Indeed she is ever intent upon pointing out that the smallest increments of time cannot be stayed. "The Second poised—debated—shot— / Another had begun" (J948). "We do not know the time we lose—," she says,

> The awful moment is
> And takes it's fundamental place
> Among the certainties. (J1106)

As stated earlier, Emily Dickinson did experience Great Time. In J765, for instance, she transfers all time systems to the person addressed.

> You constituted Time—
> I deemed Eternity
> A Revelation of Yourself—
> 'Twas therefore Deity.

And in the very first poem she bids us to "seize the one thou lovest, nor care for *space*, or *time!*" But it is abundantly clear that Emily Dickinson in the rest of her poetic career could not keep from caring for space and time. Admittedly she may have received "Bulletins all Day / From Immortality" (J827), but in the same poem she goes on to say,

> The Only Shows I see—
> Tomorrow and Today—
> Perchance Eternity.

Eternity was thus experienced on a "perchance" basis. She did not live in it but rather lived in "Tomorrow and Today," in the endless procession of passing days and seasons and running clocks, which, to her sensitive soul, must have seemed almost nightmarish. The fact that she used equestrian metaphors in describing their announcements gives an indication of the impact they had upon her. She heard them "neighing 'Day'" and in their incessant ticking she heard hoofbeats. She even fought them. Just as she arrested heavenly bodies in their courses, so she stopped clocks; but always she was forced to conclude that

> Time does go on—
> I tell it gay to those who suffer now—
> They shall survive—
> There is a sun—
> They dont believe it now. (J1121)

Not only does time pass, but it passes with bewildering speed.

> Summer is shorter than any one—
> Life is shorter than Summer—
> Seventy Years is spent as quick
> As an only Dollar. (J1506)

With her inner clock running out of control Emily Dickinson was forced to conclude that the seeming shortness of life precludes any thought or action of consequence:

> In this short Life
> That only lasts an hour
> How much—how little—is
> Within our power. (J1287)

There is still succor to be gained from Whitman's monumental victory over time, but it often seems to come when least needed, when one is predisposed to grant that neither "time nor place" avails. In more crepuscular moments, however, one is more likely to take note of Emily Dickinson's unspectacular loss. Priestly best explains why this might be true:

> We have been conditioned by thousands of years of irrational religious beliefs, myths, fairy tales, and now, in an age dominated by science and technology, we must wake up and face the truth. Passing time is all we have, and we must make the best of it. All this longing to escape from its limitation and contradictions is no better than wanting to have one's cake and yet eat it. It is desiring the impossible, and so should be rejected firmly by any mature intelligence. (p. 174)

Whitman is by no means irrelevant today—if he is, it is our fault and not his—but as far as our attitude toward time is concerned, Emily Dickinson is more our contemporary. She did not know the absurdity that we are aware of, but she realized even in her day the ineluctability of passing time. She knew it and made it known. This, says Leslie Fiedler in *No! In Thunder*, "is to give form; and to give form is to provide the possibility of delight—a delight that does not deny horror but lives at its intolerable heart." Little Emily does not shout "No!" in thunder or "affirm the void" in the modern sense of the phrase, but there is a "no" *sotto voce* in much of her poetry, delightfully rendered, which has a way of sustaining one when Thoreau's crowing like chanticleer and Whitman's roaring in the pines are cancelled out by the din of schedule-keeping modern man.

Some Features of Transformational Grammar

David Hatcher

WASHINGTON, D.C.

The first reaction to any new theory of language is almost certain to include a good deal of strong skepticism. This has unquestionably been the case with the ideas of Noam Chomsky, the M.I.T. linguist whose 1957 publication of *Syntactic Structures* marks one of the most important events in modern American linguistics. Immediately following the initial—and somewhat technical—statement of his basic theory, there were strong expressions of opinion from many quarters. As a result of the sudden and many-sided debate, several unfortunate misconceptions developed.

There were rumors that cyberneticists, in their efforts to perfect machine-translation procedures, had come upon an all-but-incomprehensible mathematical explanation of language. There was also the feeling that the "new linguistics" threatened to scuttle, wholesale, traditional language-teaching methods. Teachers of English came to dread the appearance of a new and forbidding grammar, presumably one they should know something about, and perhaps even teach.

These concerns were not too surprising. The emanations were coming from M.I.T., and the very name associated with the theory—transformational generative grammar—smelled faintly of arcane mathematics. What's more, much of the first writing on the subject was highly technical, and some of the early articles attempting to explain the theory were contradictory.

At any rate, the theory has been carefully examined—if not

attacked—ever since it was introduced. It is extremely doubtful that any theory without a solid factual foundation could have withstood this treatment for this long. Although there has been one significant revision and several minor changes, the basic theory itself has survived and become widely accepted.

The effects of the theory have been felt not only in linguistics and language study, but also in such areas as philosophy, psychology, biology, and sociology. Its influence on the teaching of English is seen in the fact that every major publisher of English grammars will soon have in print a series based on the transformationalist concept.

There is little question, then, that the theory will have an increasingly strong effect, and that the key elements of the theory will be surfacing in different disciplines. For this reason, material in the following pages will include a discussion of what appear to be some of the salient features of the theory, some of its most interesting and useful concepts. It should perhaps be admitted here that "the transformationalist" alluded to does not in fact exist anywhere. Transformationalists are people, and there are very few points on which they all would agree. Some of them would doubtless disavow statements made here about them. Nevertheless, the aspects of the theory discussed here seem to be a fair, if imperfect, representation of what this group is about, so there will be no further apologies.

The transformationalist attitude toward language study is marked by (1) primary concern with the *operations* of language, rather than with the *states* of language; (2) an attempt to develop a *generative* grammar; (3) the assumption that the most effective approach to studying language is through the use of a *model;* and (4) the concepts of the *transformation* and of *deep structure.*

Because the transformationalists have been so concerned with operations of language, some people fear an attempt to discredit the descriptivists. Chomsky, however, has explicitly recognized the contribution of this group. What the transformationalists do assert is that the study of the way language *is* can not be expected to yield as valuable information as the serious study of the way language *operates*. This attitude is related to the idea of a generative grammar, which some consider the nucleus of the theory itself.

English, like other natural languages, makes infinite use of finite means. That is, the native speaker has a finite number of entries in his vocabulary, yet he can produce an infinite number of sentences from this limited store. The process of classifying and analyzing particular sentences thus appears to have definite limits, since every sentence a reader comes across is very likely to be unique in his experience. There appears to be some validity, then, in the transformationalist's charge that linguists should go beyond attempting to describe, and should concern themselves with the regularities—or rules—which are followed in producing the sentences. The complete set of such rules—the generative grammar—sought by the transformationalists would generate all the grammatical sentences of the language, and none of the ungrammatical ones. (The term *generate* is used here in a passive sense, as in the statement that a multiplication matrix generates products.)

A statement of need for such a grammar is not a charge that descriptivists' grammars are misled. It is instead an assertion that they do not, and in fact can not, provide a full and accurate account of the innate competence, the internalized rules, of the native speaker of that language. There is no claim that the descriptivists *should* do this. It is a job chosen by the transformationalists, who seek to discover the important operations of the language, and to learn the significant rules which govern the language behavior of the native speaker-hearer. Further, the transformationalists do not limit themselves to the English language in this search. They believe that some of these rules apply to all languages, and that the discovery of such universals of language is one of their prime goals.

If they should be completely successful in this undertaking, the transformationalists will have constructed a universal grammar, one which will apply to all human languages, and which can be used to construct a specific grammar for any natural language under study. They do not claim to be on the verge of this universal grammar, nor do they claim to be around the corner from machine translation. In fact, what many consider the major contribution of the transformationalists is not in itself substantive linguistic knowledge of any kind, but is instead a method of gaining such knowledge. The method involves constructing a precise (though admittedly inadequate) model of the way language operates, and then "pushing" the model, forcing it against factual data about language. When the model fails, examination of the specific inadequacy which caused the failure will often yield information valuable not only for improving the model, but also in greater understanding of the linguistic data itself.

The validity of the approach is well established, and the job of the linguists involved with the theory is an extremely important one. It is not, however, the job of the teacher of English.

The linguists are concerned with developing a *scientific* grammar, one which provides a complete, logically verifiable explanation for the way language—any language—operates. The language teachers, on the other hand, want a *pedagogical* grammar, one which can be used in the classroom. This seems to be a reasonable division of effort among specialists in related professions; it does not automatically create opposing forces. Linguists and philosophers are principally interested in studying the underlying regularities of language. The classroom teachers, of course, are more concerned with variations—aberrations, perhaps—from the basic patterns. They want language information which seems likely to bring about improvement in the students' language usage.

Even though the purposes of the two groups differ, they are related in that any truly effective pedagogical grammar must be based on, or at least consistent with, the best available scientific grammar. For this reason, teachers of English should be somewhat familiar with the progress and the basic concepts of the theory.

One important concept of transformational grammar is that of "deep structure"—an underlying abstract linguistic structure which governs the physical form, and which also determines the semantic interpretation of the sentence. Take as an example the sentence "I speak." It is straightforward and free of complex operations, so the deep structure may be represented as identical to the written form we see.

When the complexity of the thought is increased, however, the structure must reflect this change. According to the model, kernel sentences—basic sentences such as the one above—are combined in various ways according to the governing thought. These groupings of kernel sentences are then transformed into sentences of English by rules called "transformations."

As an example of a very simple transforming operation, suppose that a speaker wants to add to the basic sentence "I speak" the idea of *emphasis*. According to the model there would be an indicator of this in the deep structure (an emphasis morpheme), and the deep structure would be represented by something like "I + emph + speak." The applicable rule would transform the emphasis morpheme into *do*, yielding "I do speak." Similarly, an interrogative morpheme would result in "Do I speak?"

Another operation of the model, one which is more complex, is embedding—planting kernel sentences inside other kernel sentences. After the embedding, transformational rules eliminate elements which are unnecessarily duplicated. This verbal telescoping can increase effectiveness, and decrease boredom, but it can also create confusion. According to the model, all structures containing such elements as adjectives and appositives are results of embedding. An example of an operation resulting in an adjective would be "Science is omniscient: Science will provide the answer::Omniscient science will provide the answer." For an appositive, the operations are: Charlie (Charlie is the chairman) is calling for order::Charlie, the chairman, is calling for order.

The usefulness of the concept of deep structure comes to light when we are working with sentences which are ambiguous, or when we are trying to represent the "same" thought in different languages.

A reasonable example of ambiguity is the sentence "I enjoy entertaining women." [1] If we move backward through the operations which could produce the sentence, we find that we have two possible deep structures, each yielding a different semantic interpretation. In the language of the transformationalists, we can not readily "recover a unique deep structure," because we find a fork in the road back, with each branch leading to a different deep structure. Some transformationalists believe that all ambiguities in English are results of irrecoverable deep structures. Whether this is true or not, the concept certainly provides an excellent pattern for dealing with the nature and source of most ambiguity. What's more, the principle seems to become more useful as the structure becomes more complex.

One of the experiences least likely to inspire hubris is that of standing before a blackboard in front of interested students, trying to deal with two sentences which seem to be parallel but which one *knows* (intuitively, perhaps) to be different, or with a single sentence which contains a subtle ambiguity. Past choices of action were usually unsatisfactory—mumbling something about "semantics" or simply ignoring the problem. Having students use the model to build a few sentences, or observe the recovery of different deep structures from physically (phonologically / graphically) identical sentences, can often not only help teachers get by such rough spots, but can also help students to understand the nature and source of ambiguity.

The transformationalists have, incidentally, provided something which the traditionalists probably appreciate—a system of diagramming. The system differs from most others in that it is

---

[1] Stolen from Professor Owen Thomas, author of *Transformational Grammar and the Teacher of English* (New York, 1965).

not primarily concerned with analysis of existing sentences. Instead, the student is given a few-word lexicon and a set of rules (for permitted operations), is told to *begin* with the concept of "sentence," and is then allowed to construct sentences himself. The purpose of this exercise is not to "teach" the student in the usual sense of the word. The transformationalist texts—the better ones, at least—are more positive than most on this point. The child is assumed to "know" his language operations in a way that he will know very few other things throughout his life. The aim of the transformationalists is to open the gates to his self-awareness, to bring the knowledge to the surface, and to permit the child to get a look at the underside of his language. Through working with the model he can learn to produce sentences which effectively express what he wants to say.

As he develops his work from the basic step to the final sentence, he reflects his progress on a "branching tree diagram," which in fact resembles an upside-down tree, the number of branches increasing with movement down to lower levels. The student sees the model in operation, and in a limited way gets to do the driving himself. While this system is still somewhat artificial, it is considerably closer to natural language activity than most.

Another matter of considerable interest to transformationalists is the question of the origin of language. Most of them view language as an integral, evolutionarily derived component of human behavior rather than something man has invented and wrapped around himself.

This is not simply an assertion that the development of man's convoluted cortex makes it possible for him to learn very complex things—including a language—but is instead a much stronger claim: that predisposition to language is a component of man's evolutionary freight, something which developed with him, and which is built into his genetic code.

There is considerable evidence for the statement that language is a part of the genetic luggage. For example, there seems to be a neurological clock—a physiological timer—which turns the language acquisition system *on* at a certain stage of human development and turns it *off* at the appropriate point farther down the line. Just as chickens deprived for the first few hours of life of the opportunity to peck are apparently incapable of being taught the skill afterward, there are indications that children deprived of language contacts beyond a certain stage are incapable of acquiring the complex of skills later.

There are other such clocks whose effects are quite apparent, such as the one which turns the reproductive capability on and off. In fact, some transformationalists believe the language acquisition phenomenon to be somehow biologically related to the reproductive capability. It is certainly analogous in that both develop with a high degree of independence of environmental factors, that they are not determined by any conscious decision on the part of the individual.

This concept of innate endowment has implications for the student of the language which go beyond the mere satisfaction of intellectual curiosity. One of the most important is that, accompanying the obvious flexibility of language, there is a characteristic systematicness which makes the flexibility possible, yet sets the limits of this flexibility.

The significance of this point of view may perhaps be better seen by contrasting it with a widely-held empiricist theory, one which views the child's mind as a *tabula rasa*, a blank slate capable of receiving whatever impressions are made upon it. The child gains language, according to this theory, by repeatedly imitating vocal sounds of his nearby elders. He later begins to associate these sounds with actions and objects. The child learns a few word-sounds, a few word-meanings, and starts out with these on a more-or-less linear life-long process of expanding and improving his communication skills.

This idea seems reasonable enough, and is apparently supported by observation. Very young children babble in a way which seems imitative, and later begin to improve their echoing after encouragement and repetition. This evidence has been enough to convince many that language is acquired through this listen-and-imitate process.

However, the *tabula rasa* idea can not stand up against mounting evidence to the contrary. One particularly telling bit of information was gained from a control group which had been overlooked for some time—children who could not hear the sounds of the adults, but who were otherwise not significantly impaired. These deaf children, it was found, babble in much the same way as do their aurally normal counterparts, and at the same stage of development. The transformationalists see this babbling as a "programmed" exercise preparing the child to participate in using a natural language. It appears that every child is capable of making, and perhaps makes, all sounds which are potentially useful in any language, without any external stimulus being required. The reinforcement and encouragement of his immediate language community will of course cause him to select (i.e., retain) the sounds and symbols of one specific language. This is a limited choice, however, a determination of which subset of the universal overlay of language is selected; the decision of greater magnitude, that of "language or no language," was made long ago in the courts of evolution.

This idea of an inborn predisposition for acquiring language is much more adequate than the *tabula rasa* concept in explaining how a child can acquire, almost as if by magic, the immensely complex set of skills needed for using language. The performance can not be duplicated by an adult, even one considerably more intelligent than the child. The adult can, of course, "learn" a language, but this is a markedly different process. A brighter-than-average father who takes his young, average son to a foreign country for a few months will lag noticeably in picking up the language.

All but the most severely retarded children acquire language, though many are incapable of learning much simpler skills which are obviously "invented" by man, and not an integral part of his mentality. A chimpanzee which can learn mechanical tricks faster than an extremely slow child will not pick up language, yet the child will.

Another bit of evidence is seen in the graph of vocabulary increase. There is a period in the life of a child during which he soaks up words at a rate which is quite unexplainable in terms of such simplistic reasons as his possession of a "curious and uncluttered mind." If for some reason his verbal contacts are limited during this period, his still uncluttered mind will not serve him nearly so well if the opportunity is provided later. He will continue to gain and lose words throughout his life, of course, but never in the same way as during this period of high absorption.

The idea of innate linguistic endowment goes a long way toward explaining how children can work these linguistic miracles; it may also provide valuable information on the related matter of what we can *not* reasonably expect people to do with language.

Many transformationalists reject the idea that the primary function of language is to provide a means of communicating with others. Some think instead that it was developed to enable man to orient himself to the world; others see it primarily as an aid to thought.

These assertions are closely related to the idea that language was evolved rather than invented, in that the most obvious justification for supposing that man invented language is that it had immediate utility for communicating. A hunting partner who could shout a warning would probably have been listed nearer the center of the cave sociogram than his mute mates.

If, on the other hand, one accepts the evolutionary development of language, then the *reasons* for its survival become important. If one major reason for the selection of language was something other than the need to communicate, then it quite possibly developed in ways which stringently limit what we can do with the language mechanism as it now exists. That is, if we can learn why and how language developed, we will be better able to decide what we can and can not do with it. This process is not quite as simple as deciding arbitrarily what we would like language to do, but it is much more likely to provide usable, realistic answers to important questions about our language.

The transformationalists, then, have made a somewhat varied contribution. They have given us the model, a methodology, and a few good ideas. Some of these ideas had been around for a long time, but had not been applied in a reasonable way to the study of language. An example of such an idea is seen in the transformationalist assertion that all absolutist assumptions—such as the invention premise—should be fair game for re-examination. This is an extremely valuable work-rule, but is after all little more than a restatement of an old principle of behavior, one which helped make well known the names of such men as Galileo, Newton, Einstein, and Planck.

Although the application of the principle to the study of human language is not likely to produce results as earth-shaking as its application to the study of physics, it has already knocked down the walls confining us to mined-out areas of study, opening access to new fields which promise the answers to more intriguing questions concerning man's language.

The Use of Biblical Allusions in Tennyson's *Harold*

Thomas G. Burton

EAST TENNESSEE STATE UNIVERSITY

Tennyson's poetic web is woven with many strands—among others, personal experience, Arthurian legend, classical myth, historical fact, scientific theory, traditional and native poetry. One diffusive and significantly-used strand in *Harold* is biblical allusion; to detect the patterns created by its use is to observe much of Tennyson's artistry.

The most significant reference to Scripture in this play appears in a statement made by Harold immediately after he has yielded to William and sworn to support the Norman Duke's claim to the English Throne:

> For having lost myself to save myself,
> Said 'ay' when I meant 'no,' lied like a lad
> That dreads the pendent scourge, said 'ay' for 'no'!
> (II.ii.355–357) [1]

Harold's words ironically reverse the meaning of the statement in its original context; Christ taught his disciples that they must sacrifice the physical self to save the spiritual: "He that findeth his life shall lose it; and he that loseth his life for my sake shall find it" (Matt. 10:39). Harold conversely sacrifices the spiritual self to save the physical. The sacrifice is not, however, for himself; Harold does not yield when Wulfnoth whispers to him: "O Harold, for my sake and for thine own!" (II.ii.333). Har-

---

[1] *The Poetic and Dramatic Works of Alfred Lord Tennyson*, ed. W. J. Rolfe (Boston and New York, 1898). Subsequent references to this edition will appear in the text.

old's "ay" still contains an "if," or is qualified, even after Wulf-noth adds: "O Harold, if thou love thine Edith, ay" (II.ii.340). It is only after Wulfnoth says, "Ay, brother—for the sake of England—ay" (II.ii.348) that Harold yields. The false oath, however, is not made entirely for the good of England; Harold says following his visions prior to the battle of Senlac Hill:

> I sware
> Falsely to him, the falser Norman, over
> His gilded ark of mummy-saints, by whom
> I knew not that I sware,—not for myself—
> For England—yet not wholly. (V.i.172–176)

The principal party, other than England, for whom Harold swears falsely is dramatically presented at this point by the entrance of Edith, at which Harold says:

> Edith, Edith,
> Get thou into thy cloister as the King
> Will'd it; be safe, the perjury-mongering Count
> Hath made too good an use of Holy Church
> To break her close! There the great God of truth
> Fill all thine hours with peace!—A lying devil
> Hath haunted me—mine oath—my wife—I fain
> Had made my marriage not a lie; I could not;
> Thou art my bride! (V.i.176–184)

This statement presents the second lie of which Harold is guilty—his marriage. Harold marries Aldwyth, the sister of Morcar (the Earl of Northumbria) and daughter of the Danish Alfgar, in order to gain the support of the North in the invasions of Norway and Normandy:

> I married her for Morcar—a sin against
> The truth of love. Evil for good, it seems,
> Is oft as childless of the good as evil
> For evil. (V.i.97–100)

This marriage, conceived by Aldwyth, is presented in biblical terms (cf. Matt. 5:9, Lev. 3:3, Lev. 16:10; italics added):

156

> *Peace-lover* is our Harold for the sake
> Of England's wholeness—so—to shake the North
> With earthquake and disruption—some division—
> Then fling mine own fair person in the gap
> A sacrifice to Harold, *a peace offering,*
> *A scapegoat marriage*—all the sins of both
> The houses on mine head—then a fair life
> And bless the Queen of England! (I.ii.113–120)

The Danes assist in the defeat of Norway, but they do not appear at Senlac to battle the Normans. Harold, therefore, has sinned against the truth of marriage in vain, a subplot that dramatically reveals the vanity of his initial lie to support William's claim for the English crown.

The lie is in fact ineffectual in regard to each of the factors for which Wulfnoth would have Harold lie. First, the lie does not save Wulfnoth. Since Wulfnoth was retained when Harold left Normandy with the words, " 'Wulfnoth is sick . . . he cannot follow' " (III.i.49), Harold must say:

> As far as touches Wulfnoth
> I that so prized plain word and naked truth
> Have sinn'd against it—all in vain.
> (III.i.53–55)

Harold's oath is also vain in regard to Edith; she is consecrated by King Edward to the church in an attempt to remove the curse of the Norman saints (III.i.156–160). When Harold responds to this plan, "No, no, no," Edward prophesies by alluding to Scripture (Matt. 26:69–75):

> Treble denial of the tongue of flesh,
> Like Peter's when he fell, and thou wilt have
> To wail for it like Peter. (III.i.161–163)

Finally, the false oath, as King Edward prophesies, does not save England:

> The green tree!
> Then a great Angel past along the highest
> Crying, 'The doom of England!' and at once

He stood beside me, in his grasp a sword [cf. Rev. 1:16]
Of lightnings, wherewithal he cleft the tree
From off the bearing trunk, and hurl'd it from him
Three fields away, and then he dash'd and drench'd,
He dyed, he soak'd the trunk with human blood,
And brought the sunder'd tree again, and set it
Straight on the trunk, that, thus baptized in blood,
Grew ever high and higher, beyond my seeing,
And shot out sidelong boughs across the deep
That dropt themselves, and rooted in far isles
Beyond my seeing; and the great Angel rose
And past again along the highest, crying,
'The doom of England!' (III.i.76–91)

This prophecy echoes the angelic visions in Revelation, especially the following one (italics added):

And the smoke of the incense, which came with the prayers of the saints, ascended up before God out of the angel's hand. And the *angel* took the censer, and filled it with fire of the altar, and *cast it into the earth:* and there were voices, and thunderings, and *lightnings,* and an earthquake. . . . The first angel sounded, and there followed hail and fire *mingled with blood,* and they were cast upon the earth: and the *third* part of *trees* was burnt up, and all *green* grass was burnt up. And the second angel sounded, and as it were a great mountain burning with fire was cast into the *sea:* and the third part of the *sea became blood* (8:4–8).

The green-tree image in Edward's vision also invites an association with a biblical use of the image, one which refers to Christ:

For, behold, the days are coming, in which they shall say . . . to the mountains, Fall on us; and to the hills, Cover us. For if they do these things in a green tree, what shall be done in the dry? (Luke 23:29–31)

These biblical passages associated with Edward's vision are not closely followed by the poet; apparently, however, they are appropriated for Tennyson's poetic purposes.

Harold's sinning against the truth is all in vain; he is defeated

for the same reason the Saxons lose to the Normans—"They
have broken the commandment of the king" (V.i.361). Even
though, as Edith states, Harold "forsware himself for all he
loved" (V.i.365), "*his* oath was broken" (V.i.362)—the man
who held "Better die than lie" (I.i.85; II.ii.154), " 'The Truth
against the World' " (II.ii.218), and "Words are the man"
(II.ii.230) lost himself to save himself.

The arrow that kills Harold is apparently the doom of God,
and the Norman monk is correct in saying:

> I am the messenger of God,
> His Norman Daniel! Mene, Mene, Tekel! [Dan. 5:25]
> Is thy wrath hell, that I should spare to cry,
> Yon Heaven is wroth with *thee?* (V.i.21–24)

Harold like Belshazzar has been weighed in the balance, found
wanting, and condemned; the monk says:

> The realm for which thou art forsworn is cursed,
> The babe enwomb'd and at the breast is cursed,
> The corpse thou whelmest with thine earth is cursed,
> The soul who fighteth on thy side is cursed,
> The seed thou sowest in thy field is cursed,
> The steer wherewith thou plowest thy field is cursed,
> The fowl that fleeth o'er thy field is cursed,
> And thou, usurper, liar. (V.i.36–43)

This curse may be compared to the biblical curse placed on
those who break "the commandments of the Lord":

> Cursed shalt thou be in the city, and cursed shalt thou be in the
> field. Cursed shall be thy basket and thy store. Cursed shall be
> the fruit of thy body, and the fruit of thy land, the increase of
> thy kine, and the flocks of thy sheep. Cursed shalt thou be when
> thou comest in, and cursed shalt thou be when thou goest out.
> The Lord shall send upon thee cursing, vexation, and rebuke,
> in all that thou settest thine hand unto for to do, until thou be
> destroyed, and until thou perish quickly. (Deut. 28:16–20)

It is also interesting to note that the curse proclaimed by the
Norman monk, which is supposedly the doom of God, echoes

Scripture; whereas the curse Harold receives from the Pope does not. However, the theme of fidelity is sustained by biblical allusion in Harold's reaction to the Pope's curse. Harold's first response is laughter, which Edith calls, "Strange and ghastly in the gloom" (III.ii.93); then he replies:

> No, not strange!
> This was old human laughter in old Rome
> Before a Pope was born, when that which reign'd
> Call'd itself God.—A kindly rendering
> Of 'Render unto Caesar.'—The Good
>   Shepherd!
> Take this, and render that. (III.ii.95–100)

Several allusions to statements of Christ are grouped in this passage: "Render therefore unto Caesar the things which are Caesar's; and unto God the things that are God's" (Matt. 22:21); "I am the good shepherd: the good shepherd giveth his life for the sheep" (John 10:11); and "thou [Peter] shalt find a piece of money: that take, and give unto them for me and thee [for the tribute]" (Matt. 17:27). By these allusions Harold tells Edith that his laughter is proper tribute to the one who like Caesar of old exalts himself as God in Rome, i.e., proper tribute to the Pope. Then Harold's allusion causes him to reflect on the irony of the Pope's being the good shepherd, who instead of like Christ dying for his sheep curses them: "William, take this 'blessed hair' (III.ii.87) of Peter and render that Anathema to Harold." The statement, however, emphasizes the theme of fidelity by suggesting indirectly that Harold is cursed because he has erred in rendering a properly balanced allegiance to England and to God.

Several other biblical allusions in the drama reiterate Harold's doom by resounding the note of judgment. Before the battle of Senlac Hill, Harold says (cf. I Cor. 15:52):

> Were the great trumpet blowing doomsday dawn,
> I needs must rest. (V.i.127)

The concluding words of the play, which allude to a statement by Cain (Gen. 4:13), also refer to the judgment of God: "My punishment is more than I can bear" (V.ii.111). Even the prefatory poem makes reference to the Judgment:

We stroll and stare
Where might made right eight hundred years ago;
Might, right? ay good, so all things make for good [cf. Rom. 8:28]—
But he and he, if soul be soul, are where
Each stands full face with all he did below. (ll.10–14)

Compare the familiar biblical statement: "For now we see through a glass, darkly; but then face to face: now I know in part; but then shall I know even as also I am known" (I Cor. 13:12).

There are many other effectively-used biblical allusions in *Harold*. Particularly interesting is King Edward's amassing of scriptural allusions; note the number in the following single speech:

It is finish'd [John 19:30].
I have built the Lord a house [I Kings 8:20]—the Lord
    hath dwelt
In darkness [I Kings 8:12]. I have built the Lord a house—
Palms, flowers [I Kings 6:29], pomegranates [I Kings 7:20], golden
    cherubim
With twenty-cubit wings from wall to wall [I Kings 6:24, 27]—
I have built the Lord a house—sing [I Chron. 25:7],
    Asaph! clash
The cymbal, Heman [I Chron. 25:1]! blow the trumpet, priest [I
    Chron. 25:5]!
Fall, cloud, and fill the house [I Kings 8:10]—lo! my two
    pillars,
Jachin and Boaz [I Kings 7:21]! (III.i.101–109)

Biblical allusion is also used for exposition; for example in the following statement by Stigand, the Archbishop of Canterbury:

Our Church in arms—the lamb the lion—not
Spear into pruning-hook—the counter way—

Cowl, helm; and crozier, battle-axe.
(V.i.249–251)

Stigand in this passage appropriates a conventional biblical metaphor for the church, the lamb (cf. John 21:15), as well as a familiar statement from Isaiah: "They shall beat their swords into plowshares, and their spears into pruninghooks" (2:4). Stigand also uses biblical allusion for description; reporting the battle to Edith, he says:

There is one
Come as Goliath [I Sam. 17:10–12] came of yore—he flings
His brand in air and catches it again,
He is chanting some old war-song. (V.i.279–282)

Edith's response sustains the figure: "And no David / To meet him?" (ll.283–284).

Biblical allusion is also used by the poet for dramatic relief and foreshadowing. At the beginning of the second act, prior to the temptation scene in which Harold is caught in William's net, the poet alludes to Scripture in the railing interchange between Harold and the Ponthieu fisherman:

Harold. Thou hast betray'd us on these rocks of thine!
Rolf. Ay, but thou liest . . . . We be fishermen; I came to see after my nets.
Harold. To drag us into them. Fishermen? devils!
Who, while ye fish for men with your false fires,
Let the great devil fish for your own souls.
Rolf. Nay then, we be liker the blessed Apostles; they were fishers of men [Matt. 4:19], Father Jean says.
Harold. I had liefer that the fish had swallowed me,
Like Jonah [Jonah 1:17], than have known there were such devils. (II.i.13–24)

It is also interesting to speculate on the possibility of several passages from the play reflecting a single biblical selection, the fifty-eighth psalm. A direct allusion is made to this psalm in a statement by Leofwin when Tostig sarcastically accuses him of playing in tune with Harold's condemnation; the statement com-

162

pares Tostig "to the deaf adder . . . that wilt not dance/ However wisely charm'd" (I.i.218–219). Compare Psalms 58: 3–5,

> The wicked are estranged from the womb: they go astray as soon as they are born, speaking lies. Their poison is like the poison of a serpent: they are like the deaf adder that stoppeth her ear; Which will not hearken to the voice of charmers, charming never so wisely.

(The reference to liars in this passage should also be noted in relation to the general theme of falsehood in the play.) There are two other passages in *Harold* that may be compared to statements in the fifty-eighth psalm. One, the statement by Aldwyth concerning her plot in Harold's absence:

> [Harold is]
> Not to come back till Tostig shall have shown
> And redden'd with his people's blood the teeth
> That shall be broken by us. (I.ii.137–139)

Compare the sixth verse of Psalm 58: "Break their teeth, O God, in their mouth: break out the great teeth of the young lions, O Lord." Also with the biblical "he shall wash his feet in the blood of the wicked" (Ps. 58:10) may be compared Wulfnoth's statement: "Our helpless folk / Are wash'd away, wailing, in their own blood" (II.ii.257–258).

References to Scripture in *Harold* are pervasive and variously used. They express and explain ideas directly and indirectly, describe events, amass to form a unified statement, provide dramatic relief, and furnish foreshadowing. The most significant use of biblical allusion, however, is in Harold's statement, which comes at the climax of the play and epitomizes perhaps the principal theme of the play—the vanity of doing evil for good:

> For having lost myself to save myself,
> Said 'ay' when I meant 'no.' (II.ii.355–356)